Praise for *Unexpected America*

"Readers' suspense is held in the unpredictable events, told in a unique alternation between formal English and slang spiced with subtle humor.

Murphy's Law…prevails again and again in struggles in Warama's personal life and financial and career hurdles that arise to be dealt with.

Warama's clever use of multiple nicknames for her characters according to their personalities or occupations—Mr. Pious, Ms. Psychologist, Mr. Savior, Mr. Millionaire, etc.—carry out the subtle humor as a secondary entertainment throughout the adventures.

…Readers will want more from this author."

-Mary Kelley, Editor for online "Live Fit Magazine"

Enjoy the read and good health.
Wanjiru W

Unexpected America

Wanjiru Warama

Athomi Books
United States of America

Unexpected America

www.WanjiruWarama.com

Published November 2016
United States of America

First Edition

ISBN: 978-0998051307

An Athomi Book
Published by Athomi Books
Lemon Grove, California, 91945
United States of America

DEDICATION

This book is dedicated to people who take
risks, for they know there are other
neighborhoods beyond their own.

CONTENTS

Chapter 1

History Echoes

Dirt-floor houses needed no vacuum cleaning or dusting. Dirt and dust were an integral part of my family's existence in Solai, Kenya. Now and then, when bits of rubbish got out of hand, and it was my turn to sweep, I held a one-gallon pot half-filled with water in my left hand and sprinkled water on the floor with the right. While the water tamed the dust, I cut leafy branches or grass, held the stems together, or bound them with a string to make a reusable broom, and swept the floor.

A high school diploma choked the peasant life I had trained for since six years old. Instead, I moved to Nairobi where I advanced to cement floors. To sweep, I armed myself with a rag, a bucket of water beside me, bent from waist, and wiped my floor to a shine. With increased upward mobility, I hired someone to bend in my stead.

Having someone do housework for me felt liberating, a milestone toward middle class in a developing country. But this changed in 1984 when my nomadic urges led me across the Atlantic Ocean to "the land of the free and the home of the brave." In America, my upward mobility stalled. Immigrants, like beggars, cannot choose. I looked for whatever could make me money for a quick getaway back to Kenya. In those days, Scripps Ranch community residents advertised in the bulletin board of the United States International University (USIU) Library, San Diego, California, for jobs that did not need work permits such as babysitter, house sitter, old folk's chauffeur, and yard work. I came across an ad for a live-in housekeeper. I grabbed it.

To stay in the USA, however, my visa required me to attend school. I applied for tuition credit, which was not hard for a former USIU student, and registered for a summer industrial psychology class.

My prospective employers, Bruce and Melanie, turned out to be a thirty-something typical middle-class American couple, with two small children—a boy and a girl. They lived in nearby Mira Mesa in a four-bedroom townhome—two bedrooms and a loft upstairs, and a bedroom downstairs. We agreed I do laundry twice a week, clean, dust, vacuum, make beds, and wash dishes daily. In exchange, I got room and board, $50 a week, and two pickups a week by Bruce from USIU when my class ended at 10:00 p.m.

I did not mention to the couple that I had never done such housekeeping before. Vacuum cleaning posed the greatest challenge. A month into the job, sweaty as I dragged their heavy wagon-like vacuum cleaner around, I thought, this housework is just like the farm-work I did in my youth, minus the scorching equatorial sun. That did not matter, though, provided I worked undercover, behind the backs of my family and people who knew me.

But my undercover plan became hard to carry out because, before long, Bruce and Melanie tweaked our verbal agreement. If they went out on a Saturday, they asked me to babysit or take the children to the community pool. I loathed the stroll through the neighborhood, white children in tow. Anyone could tell from a block away that I was a babysitter, exposing my indoor-hush-hush undertaking. But that was just a symptom. My heart agonized and ached for my daughter, Mariana. I had abdicated most of her care to a woman who worked at our house, and to my mother. And here I babysat other people's children without an idea when I would see mine.

The first Saturday I took the children swimming, the parents returned home to find their two-year-old boy with hair spiked like that of a miniature rock-star. Melanie hustled him to their bathroom. I ventured upstairs to learn how she would tame his wild hair. With a brush of water here and there, followed by palm brushes, the boy emerged as good as his old self. My African hairstyle combing, chlorine, and the sun claimed the credit for the rock-star look.

*

My employers did not complain about my work, but Melanie became a food tightwad. With the food wastage in America, I still went without food the two evenings I went to school. After Bruce picked me in his SUV, we arrived home at 10:30 p.m. He hurried upstairs to their bedroom. In minutes, the lights went out. I took my books to my bedroom before heading to the kitchen for my last chore of the day. As usual, the sink overflowed with dirty dishes, pots and pans on the counter. Except the lingering food smells, the family had consumed or discarded every morsel of food. I cleaned and went to bed without dinner.

Melanie, a registered nurse—I never learned what Bruce did—cooked in the evenings. I ate with her and the children while Bruce ate in the living room watching TV, his legs stretched on the coffee table, occasionally stroking his well-trimmed beard.

Joining the family table did not guarantee me a full stomach, either. Melanie served her six-year-old daughter twice the food she served me. The child ate half and discarded the rest. Other times, Melanie instructed her to save the leftovers in the refrigerator, only to discard it during the week. The behavior reminded me of how Kenyans accused mothers of starving their stepchildren by serving them less food than their own children.

Within one year, I hated what my life had become. Good thing my family and friends did not know of my financial bind. I could not stand the humiliation. I felt I had regressed sixteen years; that was how long it had been since I waved abject poverty goodbye. In Kenya, the poverty disease and I had separated. Its anguish confronted me only through my family. To my dismay, while in San

Diego, I realized that poverty never left me. It hovered over me like a vulture waiting to pounce on a carcass. The sad thing, though, which I did not grasp until years later, was that I had clouded my mind with worry about the humble job, losing focus of my main goal—an air ticket back to Kenya.

*

One morning, I had to change Bruce and Melanie's sheets more than the twice a week we had agreed. Melanie messed up at night as if she had slaughtered a chicken in their bed. When they woke up, instead of leaving the bedding in disarray as usual, one of them threw the top sheet and bed-cover over the bloodbath. I dared myself to make the bed without changing the bedding and see how Melanie would react—a useless indulgent thought. Instead, I clicked my tongue in irritation, yanked and rolled the sheets and fed them into the washer.

Did those bloody sheets jinx me? With washer and dryer going full blast, the house felt too warm. I opened the downstairs windows to let in the breeze, then returned to my chores, vacuum cleaning the stairwell carpeted-steps, one rung at a time. I never learned how to connect the vacuum's attachments, afraid to ask and reveal my inexperience and jeopardize my job. Vacuuming done, I dusted upstairs when I heard a swoosh sound followed by commotion. I peered from the guardrail. The sheer curtains entangled into a messy pile on the living room floor by the window. I hurried downstairs, hoping my assumption was wrong. I disentangled the curtains. My heart panicked. One of the two large—

Victorian era?—lamps had broken into dozens of pieces. I agonized what to tell Bruce and Melanie. Why did I open the windows? With my tight budget, I could not afford to replace the lamp. I straightened the mess and piled the evidence next to the side table.

That afternoon, I walked the two miles to school with a burdened heart.

My employers came up with a punishment that hurt me more than I expected. After Bruce picked me that evening, he parked in the garage and hurried into the house. By the time I reached the hallway, he sprinted up the stairs. After I dropped my books on my bed, I went to check on the status of my evidence. Nothing by the window. I proceeded to the kitchen—every piece, except the shade, rested at the bottom of the trashcan. The duo did not mention the lamp the following day—not a word. My mouth remained shut too. The guilt, however, coupled with the silent treatment, distressed me for days.

The fear of confessing a wrongdoing to a person in authority is common behavior for African children and grown-ups who grow up voiceless. They can even be wrongly accused and fail to correct the accuser. Meanwhile, they suffer in silence. But at Bruce and Melanie's I could not bear or sustain the silence. The following week, while at the dining table after dinner, I told Melanie I would look for another job.

"Okay," she said relief in her voice.

I wished she asked the reason for the notice, so I could explain. Even without further mention of the incident, somehow, I realized keeping quiet did not bode well with my character. Henceforth, I forced myself to speak up in instances I would have kept quiet before. Over the years, when members of my family gave me a dose of the timid silent treatment right in my house, I appreciated how irritating the behavior was to the person who had to put up with it. It now reminds me of a Kiswahili proverb that says, *Asiefunzwa na mama, anafunzwa na ulimwengu,* which translates to: Whoever is not taught by his/her mother will be taught by the world.

While I looked for another job, I consoled myself that, despite muddling through Bruce and Melanie's job, I had done the best I knew how. How well? They did not complain. The couple talked in one-liners. Conversations took place between Melanie and the children when they returned from day-care and before their bedtime. In the two months I worked for them, I doubt my verbal interaction with Bruce totaled ten sentences.

I now presume it was the couple's first time to hire outside help. Coupled with my negative attitude toward the job, different culture, and poor communication, a meeting of the minds had not taken place.

*

At the end of summer school, I read an ad by a single mother who needed a live-in babysitter. When we spoke, she sounded as eager to get a babysitter, as I was to get a job. Within a ten-minute phone call, she offered me the job sight unseen.

My new employer came to pick me on a Saturday, accompanied by her two sons, ages five and ten. On our way to her house, she said, "I'm happy to have an African come work for me." Then I realized why she offered me the job before we met. I did not like that at all. Usually, I endured low expectations, which gave me time to learn things, and sometimes throw in a surprise. High expectations meant little room for error.

I was not sure of the race of my new employers. The woman, at five-foot-two, medium build, and the younger boy were light brown and could pass for Arabs. The older boy had chocolate color like mine. They lived in Logan Heights, of which I had never heard. The neighborhood differed from Scripps Ranch or Mira Mesa, the only two places I had lived since I arrived in San Diego. The houses looked smaller and older—rundown, in good repair or in-between. My new employer's three-bedroom house was what they called a "shotgun house" (a term I learned later), because a person could see right through the house from the porch to the back door. The first time I saw such a floor plan was in my first school, Tindaress Primary School in Solai, Kenya.

The woman told me she was a doctor of psychology. I wondered why she bought and lived in such a humble ancient house. She later showed me another property she owned, a townhome in upscale University Town Centre, which she had moved out of and rented. She wanted to raise her boys in a black community, she said. Why old and ugly neighborhoods had to belong to black people did not make sense to me. I expected her to own a house in a neighborhood where black professionals like her lived if raising her children among her ethnic group was critical.

Well, neighborhood did not matter to me; the job did. Ms. Psychologist either failed to notice I could not cook American food, or she chose not to mention it. I faked my way through because, most times, she and the boys patronized fast-food restaurants more times than a nutritionist would have approved. I could not get away from cooking breakfast though. She wanted her children to eat cooked meals. "Full breakfast," she said.

She cooked breakfast that first Sunday I woke up in her house. I sat on a stool, by the kitchen counter, a few feet from the stove, determined to learn. Monday morning, the boys expected full breakfast, just like their mama fed them on weekends. Eggs and toast did not pose a challenge, but bacon was a different story. No one raised pigs or ate pork in Solai where I grew up. I learned of bacon when I moved to Nairobi after high school. Back then, a bacon pioneer in my family, I cooked it with oil like an omelet a handful of times and, once in a long while, ate it in restaurants.

Did the Americans cook bacon the same way I had done in Nairobi? Well, how different could it be? I placed a pan on the stove and put in two-level tablespoonsful of oil. After the oil sizzled, I spread the first bacon strip across the pan. The oil rioted—spluttered in all directions. I stood back, panicky the oil would spray the wall, my long fork in hand like a shield. After the oil calmed down, I laid bacon strips one by one, backing away after each one. In minutes, the bacon strips swam in a pan full of sputtering oil. I learned to cook bacon the authentic way by trial and error. No one called me on it.

The other thing I learned at Ms. Psychologist's was American politics. Melanie knew little of the outside world. She did not know who Nelson Mandela was or what apartheid meant. Ms. Psychologist was the opposite. After I completed my chores in the evenings, she asked me to join her in the living room so we could trade social and political insights as equals. She bombarded me with political information, which helped me have a more rounded perspective of black people in America than the criminality highlighted on TV. Because of how low I felt, however, I did not want to hear of anyone else's suffering. Nonetheless, the knowledge added to my motivation to hurry and return to Kenya, if only I could find a way to earn more money.

During the phone interview, Ms. Psychologist had asked me how much I earned per week. She matched it. With cooking included, I should have haggled for a higher pay than what Bruce and Melanie paid me. So far, my savings totaled $200. I planned to reach my target of $1200 in months as per my brain's warped belief, without any calculation. The realization kept me going, determined to return to Kenya, never to venture across any more oceans.

*

After two months at Ms. Psychologist's, her bratty boys' untamed ways had grated my mind to capacity. Spoiled sounds too mild a word to describe how they behaved. They had no regard for anybody except have their needs and wants met. I needed to change households to get peace and quiet and perhaps earn more money to reach my goal faster. I browsed for job vacancies in newspapers and magazines until a white man let me know availability of jobs did not mean one for my kind.

One want ad described a handicapped man in a wheelchair. He needed a live-in housekeeper at $100 per week. The ad did not mention cooking—peace and quiet at double the pay. When I called, the man liked that I was single with no children tagging along. I threw in my college education, to which he said, "That's great. Do you drive?"

"Yes, I drive, but I don't have a car." I tightened my grip on the receiver, my eyes shut, and waited.

"That's okay. I have a small car you can use."

Relief.

So far, we sounded a perfect match. I waited for the man to invite me for an interview while I worried what lie to tell Ms. Psychologist without raising suspicion. Instead, he asked, "When can you start?"

"I can start in a week. I need to give notice."

"That sounds reasonable. Where do you live?"

"I live in Logan Heights," I said, pride in my voice. To my foreign ears, Logan Heights sounded exotic.

"Logan Heights? Did you say Logan Heights?" he asked.

"Yes!" Is the man deaf too?

"Isn't that the black community?"

I hesitated. I did not know whose community Logan Heights belonged to. Nobody had introduced me to any black or white communities yet. This happened before Ms. Psychologist mentioned raising her children in a black community.

"Are you black?" he asked.

"I'm African … from Kenya," I said. I was not accustomed to people addressing me by my alleged skin color.

The incident jogged my memory to what I experienced when I first moved to Nairobi in 1969. Five years after independence, colonial terms like "African Estates" were still on everyone's lips. With the influx of migration to towns, Kenya outgrew residential racial profiling and embraced economic segregation instead. I had forgotten that history. Maybe America had not changed and still harbored and, on occasion, flexed its former human oppressive tendencies. I did not expect, however, such prejudice to trickle down to marginal jobs. But, it did.

Mr. Wheelchair no longer wanted my services.

The turndown hit me hard. It assaulted my ego. Not because I did not get the job, but because a disabled person in a wheelchair turned me down, who, I believed, at the basic human existence, was needier than I.

Although the man dampened my desire to look for another job, he could not close other moneymaking avenues. Before long, I became involved in an accident, which had the potential to catapult me to my goal.

Chapter 2

The Land of Milk and Honey

With my hopes for a better paying job dashed, I resolved to hunker down at Ms. Psychologist's until I saved enough money to buy that one-way ticket to Kenya. Meantime, I reflected on my experiences, mostly the bad ones, since I stepped on the American soil.

Back when I was growing up in Solai, I heard people talk or sing about "the land of milk and honey." They meant Nyeri, where Mt. Kenya looms, where my parents, their parents, and their parents' parents were born. My ancestors enjoyed four seasons, which I never experienced because by the time I came along, my parents lived under the equator sun in the Great Rift Valley.

If I could not enjoy what my parents had experienced when they were young, however, I would get a chance to do it elsewhere—in the United States of America. Through what I had heard about America, the four seasons—summer, winter, spring, and fall—were what I expected when I landed at JFK Airport in New York in 1984; cleaning and babysitting jobs unthinkable. I looked forward to a blissful stay, finish my one-year remaining to attain my bachelor's degree, and travel around the United States, the modern land of milk and honey, then return to Kenya renewed, ready for an executive job in government or in one of the multinationals in Nairobi.

But life isn't always that well packaged. I learned my first American lesson right at JFK. As I struggled to drag my luggage from the baggage area to the customs, a man rushed toward me, "Ma'am, do you need help?"

"Yes." Hard to do without men.

"That's three dollars."

"I don't have cash on me," I said. I thought he wanted to help me.

The man abandoned my luggage, flung his right arm like a fly swat toward me and said, "Forget you."

Oh, well. That is not a real man. When it happened a second time, I realized "help" had a different meaning in America.

With no help, it took me four to five stops before I reached the immigration and customs' officials. After they declared my suitcase and me clean, I rechecked the bag, and caught my flight to San Diego via St. Louis, Missouri. By then, I could hardly keep my eyelids open. When the plane arrived, I rushed to keep pace with the impatient passengers, who fumbled for their luggage in the overhead compartment. They shot out of the plane and scurried toward baggage claim as if they had an emergency awaiting their arrival. They armed themselves with carts, congregated around the luggage carousel. Others jostled to get even closer, to wait.

After I retrieved my wheel-less suitcase, I dragged it to the information desk, showed the woman my United States International University's (USIU's) instructions that said to wait for a shuttle bus. She did not seem to understand my questions. She talked with exaggerated hand gestures—a good thing since, like her, I did not understand her American English dialect. I went where she pointed and waited.

Although tired after a 30-hour travel, I felt relieved to arrive at my destination. I wished I could call my mother and tell her I had arrived in America. "America" was all she knew, and I doubt she ever learned her daughter went to a city called San Diego. People outside the United States, then and now, do not bother or know of cities and states. "America" is a catchall term. Later, I realized Americans behave the same way when they talk about going to, or wars going on in Africa, as if one country represented the whole continent.

I restrained my wondering thoughts, focused on my next move. What would I do if the shuttle bus failed to come? With no cash, where would I go? I had money all right—a cashier's check written out to United States International University. When I checked in, the school would deduct tuition, room and board, airport shuttle cost, and give me the balance. In the eighties, the Kenyan monetary system crowd did not trust its students to handle foreign currency—even a little cash for incidentals. Perhaps their monetary police feared the students might splurge before they paid their tuition or take a detour before they reached their destinations. Well, I doubt that was the reason for the dumb policy.

When the shuttle van arrived, I was the only student waiting. The driver, wearing tired work clothes, turned out to be a graduate student. He said he picked the others earlier in the evening. "Let's go," he said, picking my big suitcase. I followed him through the automatic doors to the curb where he had parked the van. He drove on Harbor Drive, along the bay. I longed to see San Diego but perhaps because of my sleepy head, coupled with the night light, I could only dimly see dozens of small boats moored at the bay. The one thing I could not miss were the streetlights, on tall lampposts with their tops curved and extended to hover over the streets like magnifying glasses. Drivers stopped as if the streetlights would issue them tickets if they failed to stop.

In the 1980s, Nairobi streets had nine-foot stumpy lampposts. At night, drivers used—they still do—stoplights like yield signs. It took another three decades for Nairobi people to see California-type traffic light posts sprout here and there.

*

The driver said the trip to campus was thirty miles, a great distance for someone without a car. That disappointed me. It sounded like country living to me—the one place I had turned my back on after I entered high school. After three months on campus, I figured he must have said thirty minutes, since the students on campus referred to distances in minutes or hours.

We took highway 163. After a long drive, the highway merged with Interstate 15 North. In minutes, we exited onto Pomerado Road east. In a quarter of a mile, we branched into a side street through an overgrowth of shrubs and a forest of eucalyptus trees. Three hundred yards ahead, I saw a scatter of earth-tone shadowy buildings blended in with the tall trees. The driver turned his head toward the buildings, "Those are the students' residences; that's where we're going." He pulled the van off the road and parked next to a concrete walkway that led to the apartments. "This is closer to your apartment; the main entrance is on other side."

It was dark everywhere except for the illumination that came from a sprinkle of lights around the buildings. We walked, our feet making crunchy noises on the walkway covered with dry eucalyptus leaves up to the steps. The four-unit, two-story apartments, with raised foundations had concrete walkways that meandered and connected the buildings. Subdued lighting came from stumpy lampposts that lined the walkways at intervals. The setup reminded me of lodges in Kenyan animal parks. During my duration on campus, I felt unsafe when I walked alone on those walkways at night, wondered whether someone lurked behind a building or in the close-by woods.

This was not the America of my dreams. Maybe my sleepy eyes tricked me—better wait until daytime to analyze the utopia I expected and looked forward to. When I say "utopia," I mean exactly that, similar to religious people and heaven. You do not have to have a clear picture of the opulence that awaits you, but you "know" and believe the only effort required on your part is to get there.

To finance my "getting there," it took me two years to gather every liquid shilling to my name. Well, I had done my part—I was in America.

The driver unlocked the door to a two-bedroom, two-bath apartment I would share with three students for the best part of a year, two to a bedroom. The bathrooms were roomy; a roommate could take a shower while the other got ready. The living room, furnished motel like—two couches, a coffee table, and four side tables—separated the two bedrooms. The driver put my suitcase on the beige-carpeted living room floor.

The man strode to the left bedroom. "I'm sure you will be happy here." He opened the door. With a sweep of his hand, he declared, "This is the bedroom you'll share with a roommate. She should be here within the week."

For whatever reason, maybe fatigue, I never felt concern about sharing a bedroom with a stranger. I just wanted to sleep.

My bedroom had a table with two chairs next to the window. There was a bunk bed with a pillow and mattress on each bed, no sheets or blankets in sight. I complained; the driver ignored me. He had done his job. "Have a good night," he said.

As the first arrival, I picked the bottom bed. Falling five feet off the top bed would not do. When my siblings and I were young, not a week went by without one of my brothers falling from the bed they shared in their cottage. One of them would report to us that the fallen continued sleeping right down where he fell on the dirt floor. The news spiced our morning entertainment when we sat around the wood fire while our mother cooked porridge.

With the right bed, I rummaged through my luggage for a wrapper to use as cover. I slumped on the bed and did not stir until daylight.

*

After the morning shower, I dressed and walked to the cafeteria, almost a quarter of a mile to the east. MacDonald Dining Hall looked impressive with high columns and glassy walls. Seated alone in one of the four-chair tables, I ate my first American meal—eggs, sausages, bread, tea, and orange juice. I looked around and wondered how, in my thirties, I would fit in with the young white people, mostly males, in the cafeteria. Well, perhaps more mature students had yet to arrive.

After breakfast, I toured the campus before I reported to the Admissions Office.

Walter Library, with columns similar to the cafeteria's, overlooked Scripps Ranch community to the north. I then realized what had duped me into believing USIU was a big-time university. The staff had plastered the impressive library and cafeteria column pictures all over their catalogue. My eyes had not tricked me the previous night. No one I knew in Kenya expected trees to be so dominant in a university campus, as if buildings were mere subjects. I had come to a backcountry university. It seemed I could not shake-off country living no matter how hard I tried.

Yards away from the library stood Legler Benbough Theatre where acting and theatre classes, shows, and meetings took place. The circular building looked small until you got inside and had to walk down stairs. Behind the theatre was four-story Daley Hall, the biggest building on campus, which housed classrooms and faculty offices. Other offices were in trailers to the east, close to the cafeteria. Farther northeast, I came to six single-story buildings connected by walkways and blended in among trees and shrubbery where students attended most of their classes.

An administrative building to the west of where the road looped back to Pomerado Road, just before the students' residence halls, housed the higher-ups—Dr. William Rust, the President; Dr. Randall Phillips, Vice-President of Student Affairs, and others.

Later, except the one swim in one of the two swimming pools, walking to classes and other activities took care of my fitness needs. With a 120-acre campus, students could hike or picnic if they did not mind military personnel in the neighboring property mistaking them for intruders, or getting hit by a stray bullet from a shooting range. This never happened, but the possibility remained. As if that were not enough, we sometime heard rattlesnakes rattle if we ventured behind some classrooms. One thing was for sure, I could not complain of dust or lack of clean air.

*

By this writing, USIU has gone through many changes. Its name changed to Alliant University. A towering Thurgood Marshall Middle School stands where students' residences used to be. The school razed the apartments and built new ones at the back of the campus. The southern road through which my van drove over thirty years ago is now a modernized street known as Novak Way. The wild trees and vegetation on its right remain intact.

The northern fork is now upgraded, lined with the world nations' flags, and is known as Avenue of Nations. The scrubby vegetation on its left remains unchanged. Other additions include a cylindrical-roofed mammoth sports center near the students' apartments, and establishment of schools of law and forensics. When I revisited the campus on January 10, 2015, I could not help but feel a tinge of envy when I saw the library laptops. When I attended, we contended with index cards.

*

Back when I arrived on the USIU campus, I dozed-off anywhere I sat or stood still. I dragged myself to my classes only to make tens of nods when seated at my desk. For the first four days, before the excessive sleep eased, I feared a tsetse fly had infected me with sleeping sickness. It was not until I met "Mr. Savior" that I learned of the term *jetlag*.

The twenty-hour-a-week work-study job I got within three weeks of my arrival was a bright spot. Based on my proficient office skills, Jack Tygett, then head of the Theatre Department, hired me in his office stationed in a trailer close to the cafeteria. The other work-study students and I did little else other than stuff envelopes. Except for a male student who asked me whether Nairobi was a civilized city, or whether there were any buildings, the rest of the crew had no time for non-work interactions. Mr. Tygett and his wing-woman demanded impeccable performance. We had to insert letters in envelopes so the recipients saw the address and the writer's name first on opening their mail.

"If you can't do it, I'll get someone who will," he once told his secretary in my presence.

It took twenty-seven years, when Mr. Tygett died in 2012, for me to learn through the newspapers of his fame as a performer and choreographer.

*

On campus, before I started the work-study job or met Mr. Savior, I became lonesome to a point of physical sickness. My "utopia" had evaporated. I did not understand the American accent and strained to communicate with fellow students. Most of them young, fresh out of high school, talked too fast, and were always in a hurry. Sometimes we conversed in class but did not say hello when we passed each other elsewhere on campus. Other foreign students seemed lost too.

The ones already acclimated—*Americanized* was the term used—acted like Americans or were too busy to spare time for new arrivals.

Teachers seemed not to understand me. When a teacher asked a question and I answered, he brushed me aside with you-don't-know-what-you-are-talking-about look, or ignored my raised hand. I did not have a woman professor until I took sociology and psychology; male professors taught business courses, the bulk of my major. I now believe the professors could not understand my accent, and it was easier to go to another student instead of straining to listen to me.

*

The one thing I remained happy about was food. I enjoyed the bounty, from chicken, beef, pork, eggs, vegetables, fruits, juices, milk, to desserts galore. The only hitch, complaints about poor cafeteria food from students never ceased. "What do you expect of cafeteria food?" or "This isn't your mother's cooking" were common retorts. Meanwhile, the wisecrackers piled their plates and glasses to the brim, and did not shy from second or third helpings. Some ate only half of their servings. The rest went to the trashcan. If a perpetrator changed his mind about food he had picked, he just trashed it and went for a different kind. Perhaps that was why the cafeteria started serving only one entrée at a time.

It stressed me to witness such waste. Granted, some food tasted bland, or too doctored with condiments like BBQ sauce, which I tasted for the first time. It took two years before my palate acclimated to American foods. But, it never became clear what students had against cafeteria food. In Kenya, students complained about weevils in their beans, half-cooked meals, too little meat or lack thereof, and minimal variety.

At USIU, males won on food wastage. But some young women couldn't stand being outshined. On Saturdays and Sundays, they came to the cafeteria clad in nylons, high-cut underwear with skimpy tops, and high heels. The young women made me uncomfortable, embarrassed for them and for myself as a woman. I suspected somebody complained because, in the next few months, the administration outlawed near-nudity in the cafeteria and classrooms.

Perhaps I should not have pointed a finger at others. I left my well-tailored modern clothes in Nairobi, and brought a paltry of casual clothes I had heard Americans associated with Africans, and which I never wore in Nairobi—like the maroon dashiki top with African prints front-and-back and wide sleeves I had worn on my flight to San Diego.

It disturbed me that, from my point of view, it had become important for me to wear what I thought Americans believed Africans wore, instead of wearing what I liked or wanted. Maybe the belief sprouted from the pictures tourists took when they went to African countries for tours. Photos of Maasai warriors or women weaving baskets, or carrying them on their heads or backs, ranked high on the camera click. Why did it not disturb me before I left

Kenya? Perhaps my new environment had jiggled something deep in my brain, thereby making me wonder about my fake existence. A life of copying others, from the food I ate, the clothes I wore, the music I listened to, and almost every aspect of my life. Nevertheless, the realization did not crystalize in my mind until I had been in the United States much longer—that, while I enjoyed the middle class status in Kenya, I slid to the bottom in the new country.

In less than a month, I believed my life was ruined. I yearned for my old life, thought of returning to Nairobi, except I lacked a return air ticket, and no rich family to finance my decisions that failed to pan out. I regretted my drastic life-altering decision. I had quit my well-paying secretarial job and diluted my relationships by my going-abroad bravado. I could have stayed in Nairobi, waded through my stressors, and completed my undergraduate program.

I professed my regret to the few African students I met. They consoled me with a story of another young woman, a daughter of one of the higher-ups in Kenya, who could not endure the American ways, especially how invisible she had become. She returned to Kenya within two weeks. The information vindicated me, gave me the right to call Americans strange with no thought of our cultural differences. I vowed to buckle up and nibble on my one-year hiatus, one day at a time.

Chapter 3

Mr. Savior

One Sunday, I hunched over my breakfast in the cafeteria, engrossed in my loneliness when footsteps I mistook for a passer-by stopped at my table. Aware of the presence, I glanced up. My mouth went agape, ashamed for someone to find me in such a depressive state. There stood a clean-cut bespectacled man, on the short side, perhaps five-foot-seven, in dressy trousers and a white shirt, sleeves folded halfway. He looked down at me. "*Wimwega?*" Hello, he said,

Did he really speak in Gikuyu?

"Are you okay?" he asked as he pulled a chair and sat across from me.

I morphed to my public persona and answered, "*Ndimwega*," I am okay.

"I didn't think you understood Gikuyu," he said.

"I do."

"Your name doesn't sound Gikuyu and you don't look like one."

"What do you mean?"

"The school must have misspelled your surname, then."

How did he know my name? "W-a-r-a-m-a is how my surname is spelled." And about not looking like a Gikuyu, I had heard that before. But I didn't care about all that small talk; I just wanted to hear him speak. In Kenya, I had never spent a day without speaking Gikuyu; speaking in English only while my thoughts swirled in my head in Gikuyu tortured me. What luck to meet a Gikuyu man in San Diego. I felt like I had met a relative, a person to converse with, consult, and help me overcome the homesickness and disorientation in which I wallowed.

The man was on the last year of his MBA program. He showed me around campus, explained the ins and outs of the various departments, and about American culture—freedom and its abuses, Hollywood, not to believe everything I saw on TV, and the country's history of oppression and its lingering relics. He also showed me how to operate the coin washer and dryer.

In Nairobi, we used cheap labor and, instead of washing machines, we hired *washing-hands*, or just did the washing ourselves. Some rich people bought washing machines for when their *washing-hands* got fed up and took off. And on the equator we needed no drying machines. The sun obliged us all year round.

My new companion became my mentor and a friend. He showed me the Von's Supermarket for when I wanted to break the monotony of cafeteria food; Kmart for any clothing or supplies I needed, and where to catch the bus for the arduous ride to downtown

San Diego. The man turned into my "savior." He wiped loneliness from my mind. I felt indebted but happy, and relaxed around him, thankful he did not bother me with men and women frolics.

Under Mr. Savior's watchful eye, my wish not to be in charge, constantly on guard, came to fruition. To my detriment, which I came to regret later, except my brief interactions with others in class, I did not make friends on campus.

*

On a Saturday afternoon, he and I walked to Von's supermarket, a quarter of a mile away, to buy toiletries and snacks. When we returned on campus, we went to his apartment. It resembled the one my roommate and I occupied—two bedrooms with a living room in-between. As a graduate student, however, he did not share his bedroom. The second bedroom belonged to a South Korean male student who seemed to have better places to spend his waking hours. With the privacy that I lacked in my apartment, Mr. Savior and I had turned his living room into our private domain.

That Saturday was no different, at least initially.

We ate fruit and other treats and traded stories about campus life. After the walk, the eats, and the afternoon chatter, I felt tired. I lay face down on the couch, my head propped on a cushion over my crossed arms. Relaxed, I became engrossed in the movie on TV. (That was another attraction to his apartment; my roommate, Jeri, and I did not own a TV.) Mr. Savior put away the rest of the shopping. After he finished, instead of returning to the smaller couch where he sat before, he came and sat below my feet.

Many times I forget the ways of men, delude myself that this one is different—he admires my wits and enjoys my company.

I never seem to learn.

Mr. Savior proved to be a typical man, just like the rest I met before, only smoother. He began to massage my feet and calves, progressed to my back and shoulders. He said people needed occasional massages to release tension. I did not doubt him. His massage complemented my relaxation, and my love-starved body enjoyed the contact. In minutes, my body became lethargic and relaxed as if it had come under the spell of a tranquilizer. On this cue, Mr. Savior scooped me with the care of one handling a newborn, walked around the coffee table, carried me into his bedroom, and deposited me on his bed.

That is how the tango between us started. Within a week, I wondered how I lived without him before. I could not get enough of the man's charisma and his smart bad-boy-persona. He interacted with other female students, giving them glances that implied he could have any of them if he so wished. Some females did not shy from hugging him in my presence, when hugs from a man seemed a form of foreplay to me. He got along well with other male students, and conversed as equals with professors on business, politics, and social issues. Some women envied me because of my caring, mature boyfriend. I did not contradict them, although I should have. My intelligent, unemotional side knew our relationship hinged on cultural compatibility, away in a foreign land.

Nonetheless, in three months, I felt reasonably happy, knew my way around campus, and practiced American ways, spelling, and terms: Don't say *biscuits*, say *cookies*; not *lift*, it's *elevator*; it's *program* not *programme*, your *mum* is *mom*, and every *woman*—strung on crack included—is a *lady*; forget that classy, well-raised nonsense. And of course, all men are *gentlemen*. I also understood my professors, some who spoke as if they had hamburgers stuck in their mouths. I had not yet joined class participation, though. Some of it sounded hollow, students talking for the sake of grades. Under Mr. Savior's tutelage and attention, American life did not seem as intimidating as before. Only one issue badgered me.

When I arrived at USIU, I paid for classes and room and board through graduation. But no money remained to pay my expenses during the upcoming six-week December holiday.

Time to go begging—Mr. Millionaire down in Florida came in handy.

Chapter 4

Mr. Millionaire

I met "Mr. Millionaire" back in Nairobi, before I came to the United States. The Service Corps of Retired Executives (SCORE) attached him to Express Kenya Ltd., the company I worked in as an administrative secretary. Besides secretary to the Financial Director, the number two to the Chief Executive Officer (CEO), I ordered stationery and printing for the company, and filled the various departments' orders every week.

The company's head office stood off Uhuru Highway, about three miles from Nairobi city center on the way to Jomo Kenyatta International Airport. The fenced-in compound had an elongated-one-floor office building at the farthest northern side. Employees parked in front while top management parked in carports at one end of the building. Across, at the opposite end, stood a huge petrol station and a garage where a throng of mechanics repaired and filled the company's big-rigs we called *Road Master*, other big and small trucks, tour vans, and sedans. The Transportation Manager in-charge of all that activity, and his secretary had offices feet away from the garage.

From my desk one late morning, I glimpsed through my office window and saw a taxi pull in front of the office building. An old white man in shorts, with stringy muscles alighted. He looked more assured than the flustered tourists who came to air their grievances when they felt wronged by the company's travel and tours department's employees in downtown Nairobi. I knew of the man; my boss had already said a consultant from the United States would be coming. The man walked down a corridor, past two Human Resource offices, before he reached my office.

Three quick knocks and my door flew open before I finished "come in." The man introduced himself. I stood to shake his hand; he towered over me. I alerted my boss on the intercom. He came out of his office to meet the consultant. The man towered over the boss too—at least by two inches. He resembled a retired football referee that I later saw on TV in America, minus the potbelly that sneaks on retired athletes.

Within a week, the man and I became office buddies. He used to own a transportation company in Florida. When he sold the company, he made a boatload of money. Tired of retirement, and with a wealth of knowledge bubbling in his head, he registered with SCORE as a transportation consultant. I do not recall how he ended at Express Kenya Ltd., but I assume it originated with my then boss, who read the Harvard Business Review the way constitutional lawyers scan the Constitution. Occasionally, SCORE ads appeared in the magazine.

Mr. Millionaire enthused about taking Express Kenya Limited to a higher profit level. Perhaps he did not know a British conglomerate owned the company's majority shares; major changes were no-starters without the parent company's approval. Like pioneers a century before him, he came equipped with supplies—toiletries and knickknacks—he needed in Nairobi, unaware he could have bought similar products locally. He also brought along Mrs. Millionaire.

The wife did not want to stay in Nairobi. Her body language objected right off the plane. When they arrived at the airport, a sea of African faces confronted her eyes beyond her expectations, no doubt making her uncomfortable. Her African knowledge before then had come from watching jumping Maasai warriors on TV nature programs or reading the National Geographic. A good American southern homemaker proved the wrong wife to take to Kenya. She boomeranged to her southern roots without even visiting the office where her husband traded his knowledge for a small stipend to cover his living expenses. Not to worry, he had three (or was it six?) months to himself without a wife underfoot.

A cheerful old fella, he wore his transportation hat with enthusiasm to match a typical CEO, then dived right in. He laughed and slapped backs of management personnel as if they were old friends, sometimes blurring business and personal. Once I saw a mid-level manager stiffen when Mr. Millionaire behaved too casually in the presence of the manager's boss.

*

Since my boss was in charge of SCORE's placement, my office became Mr. Millionaire's operation center. He must have felt isolated in the boardroom across the hall from the CEO/General Manager's office, where my boss had set him. It seemed as if he worked in my office half the time, coming in for supplies and typing services, which was a part of my job.

He also joined me for tea when I made some for my boss and me, instead of waiting for the person who made tea for the general office to serve him. He took work breaks in my office, and engaged me in office gossip. He talked about his family and life in America— nothing on social or political issues. This reinforced the general belief my fellow Kenyans and I held that everyone in America rolled in dough. He told me how hard he had worked to become a millionaire. He showed me a Boca Raton community newspaper to support his claim and, sure enough, his picture was right there on the front page.

In turn, I told him about Express Kenya Ltd., whom to kiss up to and whom to brush aside with a "Thank you for sharing" reply. He picked my brain for company information he did not want to ask my boss. We also talked about Nairobi—nothing about rural life. I did not realize then that, like others, I presented Nairobi as a representative of Kenya, and ignored the subsistence rural lifestyle led by the majority of Kenyans. I had buried that part of my life, about growing up as an indentured worker's daughter in the Rift Valley. I shared that only with people who had similar backgrounds, and even then, after they revealed parts of their stories.

*

When his assignment ended, Mr. Millionaire told me he would have preferred to stay longer, but he had to abide by SCORE rules.

Kenya had, and I suspect still has, such an effect on people— given time, it grows on you. I had noticed the effect that Mombasa, Kenya's maritime town, had on German tourists. Retired old German and other European men lived in hotels, a lifestyle they could not afford in their home countries, and romped with young local women or—covertly—men. Perhaps for the novelty of it, German writing next to Kiswahili on carts and signs had become a common sight.

*

After Mr. Millionaire left, I asked my boss how the SCORE assignment went. He shrugged it off with a backhand wave. It did not matter. Mr. Millionaire and I were not done.

Meantime, I missed his comings and goings and our chatter. I left his chair at the corner of my desk next to the wall-to-wall file shelf for a week. His presence was refreshing because people in upper management did not socialize with secretaries, always looked stern and stoic as if a relative died. Until their thoughts shifted to sexual possibilities within their grasp, typical half the time, then they begged like helpless hungry boys.

*

Back then, during my interaction with Mr. Millionaire on my home turf, I presented a happy face, but inside I buckled under my responsibilities. I was a junior at USIU, Nairobi campus. I left work at 4:00 p.m. and went to school until 10:00 p.m. My sick mother had moved in with me after my father's death in 1980. My family remained mired in poverty since most of us went to high school in mid 1960s, when my father could not afford the expenses, except a drip here and there. By the time Mother came to live with me, I felt bogged down by my siblings' needs and expectations for help, which had weighed on me progressively for over ten years. Help came in form of school fees, clothing, or worse, drop-ins for a place to eat and sleep, or to look for a job, for stretches at a time, and return bus fare. I could not even hang onto a relationship. It seemed life's misfortunes had converged on me. I worried the pressure would injure my health or cause me a mental breakdown. I knew of a student who dropped out of the university after a mental breakdown in his last year. I therefore planned to detach myself for a year—rejuvenate—while I completed my undergraduate degree elsewhere.

I applied to several foreign universities. Two replied—University of Birmingham, England and USIU, San Diego, California. My first choice was University of Birmingham, since it was closer, and, I am ashamed to admit, Kenyans still idolized Britain, a former Kenya colonizer. Birmingham University, however, required me to convert from the American curriculum I studied under to the

British system. This meant two years to finish my undergraduate degree. USIU San Diego required one year. My decision to study in the United States, and embark on a different life path, hinged on that one-year difference.

*

Before Mr. Millionaire left Nairobi, I asked him to write a letter of recommendation for me. He obliged, saying my going to the USA was a plus for Express Kenya Ltd. I had not disclosed my walk-away plan to him. By my interview date at the American Embassy, he had mailed a "To whom it may concern" letter from Boca Raton. The letter glowed with praises, vouched for my character and industry. He also attached a short cover letter, asking me to call him as soon as I arrived in San Diego. I sent him a thank-you note and promised to call him and perhaps visit him and his wife after my arrival.

At the Embassy, the interviewer seemed satisfied when he perused my finances and school and travel documents. He took it well when I told him I had taken two years to prepare, including cashing-in my retirement savings. He hesitated when he read Mr. Millionaire's praises of me. With his gaze fixed on me, over the counter, he stated he believed Mr. Millionaire was my boyfriend, and that we planned to circumvent the law. I muffled a chuckle; Mr. Millionaire could have passed for my father, if we had been from the same tribe. I was unaware at the time that he was just right under Hollywood's arm-candy standards.

I explained SCORE to the interviewer and told him how Mr. Millionaire and I met. That did not stop him from asking, "You are going to the USA to marry the man, aren't you?"

I giggled. "No. The man is happily married." To give a take-it-easy explanation, because of how stern the interviewer's face looked, I added, "Love is a strange thing. I would take advantage of it wherever I found it." It was uncharacteristic of me to talk like that to an official. The man's head moved about an inch toward me, he squinted, and looked at me for a long moment. Without another word, he raised his tooled hand and stamped APPROVED on my papers.

When I arrived in the United States, and had to deal with the American immigration personnel, I recalled with nostalgia my ignorance and innocence during the Nairobi interview. Going for an appointment at the Federal building in downtown San Diego made me feel as if I were reporting to a court of law, suspected of having committed a crime. I could either go free (get the legal authorization I needed), kept for hours if the officials deemed my answers suspicious, or go to immigration jail.

*

After my arrival in San Diego, I took a month before I called Mr. Millionaire. When in Kenya, I knew the United States was a sub-continent, but I had no perception of the distance between San Diego, California and Boca Raton, Florida, or that states were like different countries. The majority of people outside the United States, as I mentioned before, do not concern themselves with American states, cities, or their locations. Saying "going to America" suffices as if it were one big city. When I realized how far San Diego was from Boca Raton, after two phone calls, I withdrew my promise of social calls or visits—until I desperately needed help.

*

Faced with the six-week December holiday, and unable to pay for the dorms for that period, which I had not thought to budget for through sheer inexperience, I made a distress phone call to Mr. Millionaire. He picked the phone on the second ring. I put feelers first before I embarrassed myself. We spoke about my classes and reminisced about his Nairobi experience. Meanwhile, I agonized about how to tell him of my financial bind. With no alternative, my pride caved in. I stammered, looking for the right words to explain the reason for my lack of shelter. He chimed in before I finished, "That's no problem; it's about time you visited us." He promised to send me a return air ticket. All I needed was to get myself down to Boca Raton as soon my classes ended in three weeks.

Chapter 5

Boca Raton

Mr. Millionaire and his wife met me at the airport. As they approached, I wondered whether to shake their hands, as we do in Kenya, or hug them like students did at USIU campus. *Hakuna matata*, no problem. The take-charge benefactor approached, his broad smile fixed on me, "Hello, there!" He relieved me of my luggage and, with a wave of his right hand, presented his wife, who stretched her wrinkled skinny hand while she maintained eye contact. I shook her soft hand and said how nice it was to meet her. She wore a dress with tiny prints half-way-down to her shins, with a sweater draped over her shoulders. Short, five-foot-two tops, petite, fragile with blonde or grey hair, I could not tell the difference. She looked ordinary, without the "rich look" image I had conjured in my mind. Before we left the airport, and later at their residence, I caught her sneak glances at me. Perhaps her husband had oversold me, and the woman expected an executive woman. I never applied makeup in Nairobi or San Diego. That must have made me look too plain to American eyes. Well, I wore the best clothes I owned, a pair of blue jeans—popular on campus if pared with a T-shirt—and a turquoise-green top I bought at Kmart.

When we reached the parking lot, Mr. Millionaire opened their luxurious car's front passenger door. After his wife settled in, he opened the back door and shut it after I entered. I sat almost at the edge of the backseat with the door as support and placed my purse on my left side. It made me feel snug and secure. Nobody seemed to appreciate seatbelts in those days, my hosts included.

As soon as he eased the quiet car from the airport, Mr. Millionaire described everything noteworthy along our route. My mind overlooked sightseeing; it focused on how I would last for six weeks in the couple's household. I recalled how much I had enjoyed his company back in Nairobi, but in Boca Raton uneasiness unsettled me. I had never entered a white person's house before. Do they live a regular life as we do in Kenya? Will they give me a lockable bedroom so I can feel secure at night? How do they cook their food?

*

The Millionaires lived in an upstairs condominium, the Atlantic Ocean with its sprawling beaches as their backyard. He placed my luggage on the side of the foyer, close to the front door. "Welcome to our home," he said. "Let me give you a tour." We reached the first bedroom on our right. It had a bachelor-pad look, assortment of sports caps hung on a jacket stand. Menswear and suits hung in the closet like a store display. The back bedroom looked bigger with a walk-in closet full of colorful women clothing. I must have reacted.

"People don't have to sleep in the same bedroom when they get old," he said, as if talking to himself.

With separate bedrooms, and at sixty-nine, perhaps he was too old to need any. Good thing he had the ocean waves to sing him lullabies.

He described the condominium's conveniences, which included a gym, a social club, and a community room for entertaining guests. At the balcony, we savored the ocean views, captivating in the waning daylight. I almost believed the excited ocean waves signaled my welcome. From the looks of the vehicle we rode in, and the other one I saw in their underground parking, plus the almost too-beautiful-to-sit-on furniture, Mr. Millionaire had not exaggerated his financial status.

His wife called us for a drink, interrupting her husband's pleased look when he watched me intoxicated by the views and the waves. We sat at the dining table, between the living room and the kitchen. She handed us glasses of a tasty juice drink, which had a trace of mango flavor. Mr. Millionaire drank like one late for an appointment. When he finished, he softly slapped his palm on the table and said, "We should get going before it gets dark." He rose to his feet.

"Are we going somewhere else?" I asked.

"Yes, where you'll be staying."

I hurried to finish my drink. Maybe they have another residence, I thought. He did not explain. His wife said, "I hope your stay here will be pleasant. You will like Boca Raton." She did not join us.

Mr. Millionaire dragged my luggage back the way we had come—through the elevator down to the underground parking. I followed behind. In minutes, we were back on Boca Raton Streets.

Not staying in that condominium allayed my fears and discomfort, but I wondered where he was taking me. Except the Millionaires, no one in the world knew my whereabouts. Mr. Savior in San Diego only knew I went to Florida. But what could be worse? I had come all the way from Kenya, thousands of miles away.

He drove through Boca Raton, toward the interior. We passed by four beat-up single-story duplexes, which he said migrant workers occupied. In less than ten minutes, we entered a neighborhood of sprawling homes with well-trimmed hedges. He pulled his car into one of the driveways leading to an expansive ranch house with a wood-shingle roof. He parked next to a station wagon and a smaller car. He knocked on one of the double doors twice. A woman wearing shorts opened, excited as if she were waiting by the foyer. I could not determine her race. With her heavy auburn hair tied in a ponytail, she looked neither white nor black. Her exposed body, legs and arms, looked dried up like those of a desert dweller, deprived of hydration.

The three of us stood at the big foyer, exchanging greetings. "Do you prefer to shake hands or hug?" I asked the woman.

"Do whatever you feel is comfortable."

I shook her hand.

"You're cute," she said.

"I'm not sure what that means, exactly." All I had heard since I arrived in the United States was cute this and cute that, sometimes for things or people who looked downright ugly.

"You look good—that's what I mean."

"Thanks."

The way to the left led to a huge living room. She led us to the right, past the kitchen, into a family room where her family, a husband and two boys, watched TV.

I could not tell their race either. The husband had a lighter skin than his wife, but he had good dark African hair. The children had his light complexion, but had dark brown curly hair. She introduced me to her family: the skinny fourteen-year-old and his chubby twelve-year-old brother. "And I'm thirty-eight," she said. She did not tell her husband's age, but said he was an executive at IBM. The family resumed watching TV.

Mr. Millionaire helped put my luggage into a bedroom where the woman led us. He then departed after he promised to check on me the following day.

*

Mr. Millionaire and "Mrs. IBM" hung around the same community club several times a week. It seemed they enjoyed time away from their spouses. With her boys in school and her husband at work, Mrs.

IBM had turned the club into her second home. That had to be the place she and Mr. Millionaire hatched the idea and agreed on my accommodation. I had to admit, because IBMs were closer to my age, I fit in their household better than I would have in the Millionaires' condo.

I occasionally accompanied Mrs. IBM to the club where we joined Mr. Millionaire. Club activities dominated the two club groupies' interaction. They took part in club walks or runs. I then understood why they both displayed such stringy muscles. After each day's activities, which included card and other t table games for the not so agile, members socialized over a cup of tea or coffee.

Twice during my six-week stay, club members held socials where they displayed food like an art show. I had never seen such a colorful display before. Some food items emulated Christmas trees or animals and looked inedible, fit for decoration only.

Mrs. IBM thrived on rubbing shoulders with the rich members at the club. She complained her husband hated to go interact with other community residents—that all he did was play tennis or his one-man jazz band instruments set in the corner of their family room.

One evening, while Mr. IBM sorted and paid bills, Mrs. IBM wanted him to accompany her on an outing. He turned her down. I doubted he cared to accompany his know-it-all wife. When she insisted, he fired back, "What kind of husband do you want? I do what husbands do—work and provide for their families."

"That's all you talk about."

"That's not all. I also like to play tennis," he shot back.

"Work—tennis—work—tennis. Sometimes I wonder why you got married."

Mrs. IBM did not shy away from stating her wants—the flowers, fine dining, the parties, the club—a higher lifestyle than her husband provided. When Mr. Millionaire took us to dinner in an upscale restaurant by the ocean for her birthday, Mr. IBM—coming from work—insisted on parking his modest car instead of using valet parking. This evoked stares from some patrons, to his wife's embarrassment and vocal indignation. I doubted Mrs. IBM realized the people she socialized with had retired, already feathered their financial nests, while her husband still toiled in the corporate world.

Even at home, she behaved as if she would rather they ate out instead of cooking at home. They commanded a refrigerator, freezer, and a showcase pantry, but she hardily cooked the sit-down meals I associated with families. Her family scavenged for snacks when they came home. She invited me to cook whatever I wanted. Just three months in the United States, I felt shy to scrounge around her kitchen looking for familiar foods. The ones I recognized came in frozen chunks of beef, chicken, and fish, too big for me to thaw and make a meal that might have interested no one else.

I did not eat between meals or understand the constant snacks in American lives. Back in Kenya, families ate at regular set mealtimes. (Things are no doubt somewhat different today.) At the

IBMs, I settled for a butter or jam sandwich and juice or a cup of tea during the day. Many times I hungered for a wholesome meal.

When Mrs. IBM cooked for the family, she mixed several ingredients foreign to me perhaps because she pried them from cans. The meals grossed me. I ate just because my stomach craved food and did not know the difference. I loathed the mixture of tuna and mayonnaise with its gooey look, which she whipped in a bowl for a quick meal. But that was before I stayed longer in San Diego and saw potato-salad with raw onions, mayonnaise, and who knows what other stuff—and gumbo, which I could only *guess* was edible since I never tasted it.

I missed USIU cafeteria food—gasp!

Fortunately, sometimes Mr. & Mrs. Millionaire took Mr. and Mrs. IBM and me to a delicious dinner or lunch. And Christmas day of 1984, Mrs. IBM surprised me when she released the prize-winning cook in her and cooked a turkey with all the trimmings. She followed it with another surprise a few days later.

Chapter 6

Disney Whirled

One evening, the IBMs and I sat in the family room watching TV. During a commercial, Mrs. IBM announced an upcoming two-day Disney World tour for the family and me. She said she had completed hotel bookings. Her husband would drive. I wondered when she made the arrangements without me getting an inkling. Maybe Mr. IBM made them at his office.

However the trip came about, the chance to go to Disney World thrilled me. It would add to the excitement of my America stories when I returned home. I had heard of the amusement park from my boss back in Kenya. He went on a business trip to the United States and he, along with some executives at the meeting, toured Disney World. When he returned, he wrote an article about his wonderful experience and got it published by the Daily Nation Newspaper. Despite all that, I offered to stay home, not to impose on them. "N-o-o-o-o," the family said in unison.

"Everything is paid for, no point in wasting money," Mrs. IBM said.

We left for Disney World, Orlando, Florida the following weekend.

Mr. IBM paid for our park entrance fees. We gathered a few yards from the gate to highlight our activity preferences on the park's map. After we agreed on a central meeting place in case we got separated, he said they budgeted to pay for my park entrance fee and the generic rides included, hotel room, and dinner. "Lunch or anything personal you buy will be on you," he said.

His announcement made me feel inadequate, like a dependent child. That was exactly why I wanted the family to visit the amusement park without me. I appreciated the IBMs' generosity, but they should have consulted me before they included me.

The day after Mr. Millionaire deposited me at their house, without my prior knowledge, I had projected how I wanted to spend my time. Tour the local library—I did not step-in there even once—and read books, walk around the neighborhood, watch TV, and enjoy an occasional swim in their backyard pool. I looked forward to coasting along for the six weeks.

My conservative agenda came about because, in addition to $80 in my pocket, my bank account held only an amount to buy books for my final semester, about $200 for necessities, and the $50 minimum balance the bank required to maintain the account. Fortunately, I had paid my campus room and board up to graduation. How to raise money for my return ticket to Kenya remained a mystery. I therefore needed to hang onto every penny I had. Disney

World trinkets and lunches were a luxury I did not need. With free dinner and the hotel's continental breakfast, however, I managed okay. But, just to show I could be self-reliant, I threw in a little snack during the day.

This was my first visit to an amusement park, and I did not want to waste a minute sulking or worrying about budgets. I shelved my stress and joined the family in the fun. We exhausted ourselves taking different rides, the scarier the merrier. A group of others and I rode in a miniature bullet train, which wove through a pitch-dark tube at body-breaking speed. Screams of exhilaration and fear surrounded me—hard to distinguish between the two. I did not scream, kept my mouth shut to contain my riotous insides. My spooked heart rammed on my chest and threatened to burst from the pressure. Crunched, I held on—the alternative unthinkable. When my feet touched the ground at the other end, I swore off theme-park rides for the rest of my days. Thirty-one years later, the vow remains unbroken.

That first evening we could not wait to finish dinner and rush to our hotel room to share our day's exploits. We occupied a double room where the boys slept in sleeping bags on the floor, Mr. & Mrs. IBM slept in a queen-size bed and I in the smaller one. At the room, someone switched on the TV. We did not pay attention. We traded stories—talked over each other—about the scary rides and the day's memorable experiences. Caught up in the excitement as she narrated how she enjoyed the day, Mrs. IBM said, "If it weren't for Mr. Millionaire, we couldn't afford this trip."

The whole room got quiet. I waited for a reaction, in hopes I was not the only one ignorant of that fact. No one acted surprised, asked a question, or made a comment.

Before I fell asleep that evening, I thought about my station in life. It seemed I had no place or a group I fit in before something cropped up to bother me. Except for Mr. Savior's company in San Diego, my stress rivalled what made me leave Kenya.

*

By the time we returned to Boca Raton, I had stopped beating on myself when I wondered about what brings happiness. When I first came to the IBMs' house, I thought they had nothing to worry them. They had intelligent, healthy children, food galore, his and hers room-size closets full of fashionable clothes, a sprawling home with everything a person could desire. Yet they did not behave or appear happy. I sensed their strained relationship in the first two weeks and confirmed it after an incident I witnessed which may or may not be proof.

One night, an urge hit me at about 3:00 a.m. Without a bathroom off my bedroom, I debated whether to hold it in until dawn. Going won. I felt my way in the dark and opened the door. Enough light illuminated from the backyard through the glass wall that ran across the kitchen and family room. At the door, I turned left to walk to the bathroom that faced the family room. Just before

I reached the bathroom door, I turned when I felt a presence on my right. A seated silhouette startled me. I must have reacted because the form turned with a start. It turned out to be Mr. IBM, seated in his recliner chair, exactly where I left him watching TV earlier that night. Embarrassed, I hurried. He had disappeared when I came out of the bathroom.

Even my benefactor, Mr. Millionaire, with all his money, could not claim contentment. He coasted in a web many men find themselves in when they reach their golden years. He swung between a long-term marriage, etched in steel, and a natural need to appease his sexual urges. Urges most likely his wife, like many women without hormonal replacement, could not entertain after her estrogen depletion. Since we met in Nairobi, I could have sworn he never gravitated toward illicit sexual tendencies. That his paying for my air ticket, accommodation at the IBMs, and a trip to Disney World stemmed from his kindness and financial surplus. He proved that a man might never wholeheartedly embrace sexual retirement, even after his beloved equipment fails him.

*

Sometimes Mr. Millionaire dropped in at the IBM's house during the day. If Mrs. IBM was home, he said, "I just wanted to check on you girls." He chatted for a few minutes, turned down the drink she offered him, and left. If he found me alone, a nightclub bouncer could not have dragged him out; he aimed to get me into my bedroom. If Mrs. IBM returned and found him visiting, he claimed he came to keep me company. Not privy to his covert behavior, she thanked him for his kindness and concern for the African visitor.

It had started slowly, he tickling me like I were a child, just a week after he and his wife picked me from the airport.

His passes had me at a loss. I avoided being alone with him, lied that Mrs. IBM would return soon, dashed away or struggled to get away when he caught me unawares in the backyard. This happened because we left the front door unlocked unless no one was home. If he came, knocked several times and nobody answered, he came right in. If I heard a knock while in the family room or bedroom, I rushed, peered through the peephole and secured the door fast if it turned out to be him.

With his big mouth—millionaire this, millionaire that—I thought he should have considered the money he spent on me as a donation—okay, charity—and not expect extra benefits beyond friendship. Back when we met at Express Kenya Ltd. in Nairobi, I waited on him at least an hour every day—besides social interactions—five days a week, for months. Half of what I did had nothing to do with my job, except to make him comfortable away from home. But at his home turf, he wanted to change the implied terms of our friendship.

I counted days to my upcoming flight back to San Diego, thankful my airline ticket remained tucked away in a safe place. I felt disheartened that my six-weeks in Boca Raton had not resulted in any real connection with the IBMs. And the Millionaires' friendship, which I believed would thrive after my visit, had cracked.

The unsettled part was who to drive me to the airport. I hoped Mrs. IBM volunteered. She had played the biggest part of my six-week stay—even lent me a dress to wear to nicer outings. Once, she asked me to accompany her on a drive to Miami for personal business. I do not recall what she had to do there, but it was a treat for me, and an addition to my take-home stories' arsenal.

I found no effective way to communicate my preference to her without her wanting to know the reason. Knowing her vocal personality, I feared she would ask Mr. Millionaire. It would have then come down to my word against his, spattering bad feelings all around.

So, I kept my mouth shut, let his behavior become another wayward man-secret to keep, like the other married men's secrets I had kept, concerned about their innocent wives, and what damage the men's wandering-eye and groping childish behavior disclosure would do to their standing in their families and communities.

*

When the Millionaires took my host family and me to one final dinner before I left the Sunshine State, the mode of my transportation to the airport came up in our discussion. He, used to getting his way, beat Mrs. IBM on the airport run. I did not fret. He could do little between the house and the airport.

On the airport drive, he became tongue-tied, uncharacteristic for him. Nonetheless, he communicated what he wanted done. As he drove, his right hand held my left hand, showed he would settle for my hand—better than nothing. With ambivalence, my hand hesitantly agreed, crept toward the target, knocked—no one home. In January of 1985, Viagra had not come in yet. My hand could not help him, and neither could it help our friendship, which slipped out the window and he slipped out of my life.

Chapter 7

Men, Men, Men!

Before I went to Florida, my well-mannered ballerina roommate Jeri, whose parents would have been proud of the great job they had done in raising her, invited me to accompany her and her friends to a club to celebrate her twenty-first birthday. I wore a full-length African-style green, two-piece outfit that made me not only look exotic but also feel like a chaperone to the mostly young patrons. Some of them looked half my age. The DJ played music I never heard before. Unbeknownst to me, most of the music we liked and boogied to in Kenya in the 1970s was by black artists.

At the club, no one paid cover charge or bought a drink for another, unlike in Kenya where friends took turns to buy drinks for members in their group. In San Diego, patrons who were not dancing leaned on walls or stood in groups nursing their drinks. If one of them needed a refill, he disappeared and reappeared, drink in hand.

It was nice to see Jeri dressed up. On campus, she wore sweat pants, hauled an oversized duffel bag, and seemed busy-busy almost every day. When she moved in as my roommate and introduced herself as a ballet dancer, I wondered whether she could make a living out of twirling around. Coming from Kenya, I put ballet into the sports category—an activity or a hobby one did on the side, not a career.

Before graduation, Jeri invited me to her ballet solo routine at a musical held at Langley Hall on campus. I went out of courtesy and curiosity to see how she danced with those deformed-looking shoes she heaped in one corner of our bedroom.

When the time came for her segment, she trotted from behind the curtain, adorned in a circular white dress that made her look like a floating angel while she danced. It was a captivating routine, my first ballet watch. That evening's experience made me feel as if I had been on a pleasant journey in a hitherto unknown wonderland.

*

For the nine months Jeri and I shared an apartment, not once did she behave out of line or irritate me. But she was young, white, and majoring in something alien to me—not great ingredients for the college friendship I needed. There were few mature women on campus—typical in college boomerangs.

The African male student population was higher. Mr. Savior did not trust them. If I found a man visiting him in his apartment, he told me, "Can you come later after we finish here?" If a man found us together, Mr. Savior introduced us but hogged the conversation to ensure there was no interaction between the man and me. The only man he did not mind was my friend Qui, a petite Vietnamese who visited us at Mr. Savior's or came to socialize in my apartment, or I in his.

Perhaps to explain his distrust for his friends or acquaintances, Mr. Savior spoke of how precarious campus life could be for women. He told me of a woman who was gang-raped by three African students. I later met her during our graduation ceremony. Mr. Savior did not disclose the men's names or what countries they came from. The woman planned to report the incident to school authorities, but he and other "respected" African men intervened and discouraged her. They told her she would forever shoulder the responsibility of destroying three men's lives. The woman gave in after she weighed which was a heavier burden to bear: rape or three destroyed lives.

We, the women on campus, had to beware to avoid similar fate. The mature men students I met displayed mannerisms similar to those of incarcerated men, ogled women with unmistakable hunger. I never dared mention to Mr. Savior the passes some of the men made, one Cameroonian harping on me the longest. Nevertheless, I counted myself lucky to have a boyfriend to discourage the men until one of them tried to rape me. I did not tell Mr. Savior. If I told him that the doctoral student walked with me from the library and invited me to stop at his apartment, ostensibly to finish discussing college programs we were talking about, and then attacking me, Mr. Savior would still have blamed me for entering the man's apartment.

From my previous interactions with men in Kenya, a story for another book, I now believe those mature men on campus had grown accustomed to women's submission in their home countries, their societies' benign outlook on rape, and poor treatment of women. Most likely, the men held senior jobs, and perhaps their studies abroad helped them change careers or upgrade their professions. Before I graduated, a Kenyan former foreign minister, a practicing psychiatrist, came on campus to study psychology. Unlike many others, he had money to rent an off-campus apartment and bring his wife along.

Young men did not seem that needy; they took life in stride, mixed, and made friends readily.

*

I still failed to appreciate how much Mr. Savior loathed me socializing with men, no matter how innocent the exchange, until one Friday afternoon after class. I strolled from the library accompanied by two doctoral students, one of whom spoke about London with the admiration of a native. The two men said they headed to downtown San Diego for sightseeing. "You can join us if you like," Mr. Londoner said. I jumped at the offer. He was Mr. Savior's friend, and I believed his company acceptable. I never wanted to put myself in company of men unless I knew them well. Besides safety, Mr. Savior would have accused me of flirting with other men.

My enthusiasm was reasonable. In six months, I had gone downtown only once—on a two-hour bus ride—the first month I arrived on campus, just to know or brag I had been to the city. I had walked about a mile to catch that bus because buses never entered the sprawling USIU campus back then. When I entered the air-conditioned bus, I rushed and sat down as it pulled off the bus stop. I raked in my handbag, then held in my hand currency I didn't understand, waiting for the bus conductor to come take his share. Instead, a baritone voice brought me to attention. "Lady! You can't ride a bus without paying," the driver said.

I fidgeted, looked up and down the aisle, embarrassed and confused, wondered what he wanted me to do. Uneasiness settled in the bus before it became clear the world is full of good people. A young woman from two seats behind rushed to my side, sorted the coins in my hand, and said, "Come." I followed her. We each grabbed a seat frame at a time to steady ourselves. At the front of the bus, the woman held onto a bar around a boxy stand by the driver. She inserted my coins into the receptacle, "This is where you put your exact fare before you sit down," she said.

*

Mr. Londoner led his friend and me to a four-door metallic dark-blue car parked near the residence halls. I got in the backseat. The two men sat in front. We took Highway 163 South. Just before downtown, the highway narrowed into two lanes and cut through

Balboa Park, like going through a tamed forest with trees on both sides, and in the middle of the dual parkway.

We meandered around the business district to see its then few high-rises before we drove on Harbor Drive, along the San Diego Bay. Mr. Londoner showed us the various highlights like the County Administration Building, where I would work fourteen years later. San Diego looked just like any other city, but the bay looked more inviting, littered with different boat sizes. Citizens could enjoy scenic walks, hang around, or grab something to eat.

Mombasa, the one city in Kenya, which would have a great scenic drive, has its beaches privately owned by hotels that line the coast like little dominions, some of them with cabanas only yards away from the public white sand. These hotels cater to tourists or the upper class. Back in the eighties—which may still be the case—the masses contended with one or two designated public beaches that they reached by passing tacky run-down kiosks selling soda and snacks.

Our San Diego tour took about two hours without a drink stop.

After Mr. Londoner dropped me off before he parked his car, I stopped at my apartment, dropped my books on the table, and hurried to Mr. Savior's apartment. I could not wait to tell him I had finally toured the city. When he opened the door, he growled at me, "I've been looking for you everywhere. Where were you?"

"I went sightseeing with Mr. Londoner and his friend," I said, walking toward the couch, convinced the story I was about to tell him would calm him. He shifted, planted himself between the couch and me. I looked at his face—it had turned a shade darker. His lips twitched. "How could you go out with men without my knowledge?"

My smile disappeared, sightseeing euphoria pre-empted. "Mr. Londoner is your friend," I ventured, hoping that would sooth him.

"I don't care whether he is my friend or not..." followed with a snappy right backhand to my temple.

I swayed, gasped in shock.

The man slapped and kicked. I was up. I was down. At one time, laid on my side, he made as if to bite my shoulder. When his open mouth got close, he instead clenched his teeth so hard his face shook. I did not retaliate, claw his face or throw a single sissy-punch. I let him rough me up—my mind blank. Even my father's advice, to my mother's chagrin when I was nine years old, remained dormant in my subconscious mind.

"If a person attacks you, defend yourself," he had said. "If the person is bigger than you, pick a weapon. Cut him with a machete if you have to."

It had been too long since my father's tutelage, but my survival instinct kicked in and obliterated my initial shock. As I lay down on the carpet, I saw Mr. Savior ready to come down on me with his elbow, wrestler-style. I shifted my upper body with just a second to spare, thanks to those wrestling matches my friends and I had watched, congregated in our house in Nairobi every Monday evening. The man collected himself from his wrestler miss and hovered over me. Fearlessness took over my body. Still as a statue, I gazed up at him. He seemed insane, oblivious to his actions. But the fall must have shaken him. He paused for a long moment and looked down at me as if coming out of a trance. I maintained my stare—without blinking. The murderous look on his face faded, replaced by revulsion. He grabbed my right arm, dragged me onto the steps outside his door, and kicked me out as they do in alley bars. "Get out! I don't want to see you ever again!" He slammed the door shut.

Darkness had come in except for the lighting on the walkways around the apartments. I fumbled, steadied myself, shuffled, anxious to get to my apartment before anyone saw me. I worried somebody may have heard the commotion, but thankful no one witnessed it. When I entered my apartment, I sighed with relief. Jeri was not in to see me in my roughed state. I did not think to check for any damage on my body before I slipped into my bed fast, fully clothed.

When I awoke Saturday morning, my body ached as if I dug ditches all night long. My self-esteem wallowed in the dumps, but my body had no bruises my dark hue could not conceal. My heart hungered to talk to someone. I had no one with whom to share my sorrow. Unless in class, at the library, or at work-study, I had spent all my free time with Mr. Savior. Loneliness returned with a vengeance.

I picked at my food that weekend, tossed and turned at night, and did not study. My body dragged about like a zombie, brushing aside any break-up possibility. I could not go on without Mr. Savior. The man came into my life just six months earlier and now he had beaten me as if he were defending himself from an attacker. But that didn't diminish my craving for him. He did not intend to assault me, he just made a mistake, I told myself, overlooking his mean streak I had noted a while back.

*

One time he told me about a man who had been worried silly when his girlfriend became pregnant. Mr. Savior said he did not understand the big fuss.

"What do you mean?" I asked.

"The man is a wimp."

"For being concerned about an unplanned pregnancy?"

"He needs to decide and move on."

"What would you do?"

"Simple. She would get an abortion."

"She might want to keep the baby," I said.

He snickered. "I would get rid of it myself. I'll never have an illegitimate child."

Back then, I had lowered my eyes, saying nothing, thinking his meanness had nothing to do with me. But this beating had to do with me. I needed to take action. It never occurred to me that Mr. Savior needed to do anything.

By Sunday, my mind resolved to apologize—for what, I had no clue, and it did not matter. An apology would give me a chance to win my lover back. My pride would not let me contact him in person. But the truth, I feared how he would react.

I wrote an apology for going out without his knowledge. I said it was inconsiderate of me to make him worry about me. Did he worry that a mugger would attack me out there? Hardly. I knew concern for me was not the reason. He was a jealous predator, similar to all the other children and wife beaters, both men and women, who seem to worry about their relatives' safety while they, the beaters, are the actual threats living in the homes, from whom the relatives need to shield themselves. I shared a bed with one. And, like any assaulter, he didn't see the contradiction. Anyway, on my way to dinner, I stuck my apology letter in my jeans pocket, unsure how to deliver it. At the cafeteria, I approached a young man whom Mr. Savior and I knew. I gave him the letter and satisfied his questioning look with, "'Mr. Savior' is upset with me."

The following day, Monday, Mr. Savior did not reply to my letter—he never put such exchanges in writing. He sent the young man to tell me to pass by his apartment before dinner.

As I walked there, I feared what he might do, but my need for him and the hope he might take me back outweighed my fear. When he opened the door, he said, "So, you decided to put our business out on the street?"

Oh, my! I did not expect such a question. His tone of voice was accusatory but non-confrontational. "That's why I wrote the letter—I know better than to confide in the young man."
I watched his face for a reaction.

"Ummmm…" he said and then paused as if in contemplation. He broke the silence. "Can I offer you a drink?"

"Not right now." What a chameleon monster!

"Do you want to join me for a walk before dinner?"

"Y-e-s," I said, surprised how easily he rolled over.

"Okay, let's go."

We walked, sprinted, strolled, as if the beating never happened. It remained unmentioned until I disclosed it in this book.

Our relationship went back on. I turned into a victim, could not envision my life without Mr. Savior. If the letter I wrote had not satisfied him, and he told me to write a longer one, to prove my sincere apology, I would have gladly done so. Perhaps even promise I would never, ever look or talk to another man.

But to protect my dumb side, when my brain and heart do stupid things, my body system balances itself. Besides, it never forgets or forgives an attacker. It first waits for my brain to acknowledge the mistake and make amends. Then it nudges my heart to choke that silly "but I love him" claim that desperate or weak women throw around when they are dependent and fear facing life alone.

That time, my body waited for a month. Thereafter, it shut down its response mechanism, cell by cell. Mr. Savior's caress felt like a stranger's inappropriate touch. His come-hither advances started to irritate me. When I gave in, my body did not cooperate but lay there like a log. My relationship eyes shed their cataracts; they scanned his actions while my brain processed and analyzed them, past and present. My reasoning powers returned and poked holes into my victim's mind-set, one thought at a time.

From the four to five times a week I spent the night with my attacker, I cut back one sleepover every week. In a month, I slept in his bed once a week, or two when he pressed me. I promised myself to beware of Mr. Savior's type of men—old country, new country, same problem. Blame that abusive relationship on loneliness. Perhaps to avoid self-blame? Nature or nurture, it is the way of subservient human beings, who lack self-confidence, women in particular.

I have no book knowledge on psycho-victim relationships, and I do not want to sound preachy. But I believe when you have a psycho on your hands—man or woman—you should be careful not to clue him or her about any imminent breakup. You might get maimed, killed, or whatever else, even with a court's restraining order right in your pocket. Breakups are not in their vocabulary; neither is reasoning. If your predator has nothing to lose or is past caring, disappear to some safe house, or leave town while you still have your life. If he commits his terrors under wraps so that anyone who knows him remains ignorant about that side of him, just ease out—use a ton of reasons to get out of the house or his company—get busy, get sick, or visit family. You might get lucky, and the predator might dump you and you will be home free.

Mr. Savior was a clean-cut, "pillar-of-the-community" kind of man. I took four months to ease out of his life, unaware it would take another seven years for a complete severance.

*

Whether he ever regretted his behavior, I could not tell you. He threw me an occasional accusatory side-glance about my cold response to his advances, but never complained. We coasted along until our graduation day. That was the relationship cutoff date I had set, as soon as I moved off campus.

Graduation day came—he earned his MBA, and I completed my Bachelors. I hungered for my family members to be present to root for me at the ceremony, held at the San Diego Civic Center. Some students received thunderous hollers and claps from their families and friends when they walked to the podium to collect their imitation cylindrical diplomas from Dr. William Rust, USIU President. (Students collected the actual diplomas from school afterward.) For graduates without families like me, few faculty members and classmates did the honors. But they couldn't match the flowers, the balloons, the hugs, or the chatter the popular students received.

Mr. Savior and Kathy, a woman who volunteered on campus and hosted foreign students on occasion, had scheduled a party allegedly for him and me. They held the party at her house in Scripps

Ranch where she lived with her husband and two small sons. Without money to contribute, I remained on the sidelines during the arrangements. It became his party, with me as a footnote. Twice Kathy reminded guests, "Wanjiru graduated today, too."

"I wish my mother were here," I said. Kathy's mother, Nancy, must have had pity on me. She agreed to volunteer to fill-in as my surrogate mother during the photo shoot. While she and I talked, sitting on the couch in the family room, in a moment of relaxed bonding, and without malice, she said, "I had no idea Africans went to college."

What is new?

One guest at the party dropped me back on campus before the party wrapped up. I walked to a payphone by the pool, called our neighbor in Nairobi, who lived a block away from my family. I told him to send someone to tell my mother to go wait for my phone call at his house. She could not afford and did not need a telephone after I left Nairobi. My mother waited for my call for over an hour. Meantime, I dialed the neighbor's phone number, at intervals. By the time my second call went through, my mother had given up waiting and returned home. On my way back to my apartment, I regretted one more time leaving Nairobi. I missed everything and everyone I ran to a foreign county to take a break from. I indulged in a private cry.

I never got another chance to call or speak to my mother.

Two months after graduation, I sent her a passport-size photo. In an enclosed letter, I told her I would take the rest of the graduation photos with me when I returned to Kenya. She must have wondered why I took that long to send a photo and why I had not returned home. But Mother had confidence in me. Anytime she had no idea what I was up to, she believed there was a sound undisclosed reason, which I would tell her in time. Her time ran out before she learned how simple my reason was: to work and raise enough money for my air ticket to Kenya.

Chapter 8

Accident

Earning enough money to buy an air ticket back to Kenya took over my life, especially when I accepted that it would take much longer after a disabled white man turned me down for a job, simply because I am an African. As if that did not worry me enough, a city bus I rode in one late summer afternoon of 1985 got into an accident. I then worked on my second hush-hush job—housekeeper/babysitter—for Ms. Psychologist.

The bus cruised west on La Jolla Village Drive, after leaving University Towne Centre (UTC). I sat on the second seat behind the driver, on the aisle side. Before the bus crossed Highway 5 overpass, a small white car appeared, exiting highway 5 south at high speed. The bus driver slowed then sped up, perhaps to teach a lesson to the small car's driver.

Unable to stop before entering La Jolla Village Drive, the car breezed through the stop sign. Critical mass! The bus driver braked hard. I jerked forward; my head hit my hands, which gripped the front seat frame. He swerved the steering wheel to the left. The bus zoomed over the street divider. Just before we dived into Highway 5 below, the bus swerved right. It ploughed through a light pole, shrubs, and flattened vegetation in its wake. When the bus stabilized, the small car had disappeared; the driver remained alone with about a dozen rattled passengers.

The police arrived in minutes and found us standing by the bus. Some people still looked dazed, others—like me—anxious but quiet, and some complained to the driver that they would be late wherever they headed. The officers took passengers' details—names, addresses, and where each passenger sat in the bus. The driver and passengers heaped blame on the long-gone car's driver. He did not mention the part he played, without which there would not have been an accident. The police suggested a hospital check-up. I was so rattled I turned it down, just wanted to go home, like a child going to mama. I rode home in the replacement bus the Metropolitan Transit Service sent.

The following day my body ached like I shot out of a cannon. It pained me to turn my neck to the right. The way things stood, I might return to Kenya crippled. But no doctor or hospital for me, though. My $200 stash would remain untouched, no matter what. I did not yet know about low-income city clinics.

Ms. Psychologist said the bus company needed to pay my medical expenses and suggested I go to an emergency room. She directed me where to find one close by. I walked there. Seated were about five of the poorest among us crowd—tired clothes and hunched shoulders. It is funny how I never had the slightest inclination I could be one of them.

The X-rays showed I suffered overstretched ligaments and traumatized muscles, but no broken bones. The doctor prescribed a neck support for the next two weeks.

Within the week, a man called from an insurance company. I now guess they wanted to reach me before a member of the legal crowd did, although I did not know about ambulance chasers at the time. The insurance rep arrived at Ms. Psychologist's house mid-morning, suited in a long-sleeved white shirt and tie—no jacket. He said his company would compensate me for missed workdays. He never asked how the accident occurred or mentioned medical expenses. I did not fret. If the company paid me, I would buy that one-way ticket to Kenya and nurse my muscles when I arrived home.

If I were in Kenya, my lawyer cousin would have reproached me for those stifling peasant thoughts. Instead, with all the money struggles that dogged me, he perhaps would have advised me to hobble, cane in hand, to a member of the San Diego legal custodians. On arrival to the office, slur my words and beg their help to leech on the insurance company's deep pockets.

"How much do you make a month?" the insurance man asked.

I hesitated, embarrassed how little my time was worth. "I'm paid weekly—$50."

He scribbled on his clipboard. "I'll recommend my company pay you at least a month's wages, plus something for your pain and suffering."

"Oh," I said, making a fast calculation in my head. $200? Not enough to get me back to the cradle.

"How much do you think the company should pay you?"

I hesitated again. With no point of reference, I wondered how much to ask. How much was pain and suffering? I recalled my cousin had said that depended on someone's age and current or future earning capacity, at least in Kenya. Better ask for more and be haggled down, my peasant brain reasoned. It took another five years before I learned it was bad business to mention a figure before an offer. But back then, I settled on a figure I thought the company could bear. "$700," I said.

Mr. Insurance did not acknowledge the $700. Perhaps I should have asked for less—$600, maybe. Suspense reigned over me as the man scribbled on his clipboard. "I'll recommend the company pay you $800."

"Okay," I said, restraining my excitement. With such an amount, I would savor my mother's cooking in four months.

He promised to contact me as soon as his company prepared an agreement and a check to settle the accident claim—a claim I had not even filed. Yoo-hoo!

I expected Mr. Insurance to leave, but he remained seated. I did not mind. For a live-in babysitter with a sore neck, I could use some company.

The man asked about wars, culture—housing, food, clothing, education, climate in Africa—the whole shebang. He breezed through my answers with no follow-up questions. Perhaps because it was his first time to meet a typical woman fresh from the slighted, maligned, and abused low-self-esteem continent.

Finally, he asked the one question I guessed must have itched him—polygamy. He wanted to know the African men's secret. "How do they marry multiple wives?" he asked. "Why do the women allow it?"

Trying to explain African polygamy and its many layers is a book-long story. The question, however, beat the ones people asked me about civilization, for which I had not honed an acceptable answer. On polygamy, I should have referred Mr. Insurance to the State of Utah, United States, but I did not know about Utah and its dance with polygamy then. Instead, I told him that most men were incorrigible polygamists—Africans, Americans, Europeans, Asians, the whole lot.

The man looked at me, squinted, perhaps thinking, how dare you include American men with the lowlife polygamists? "It's illegal for Americans to marry multiple wives."

"Legal or illegal depends on a group's interpretation," I said.

"What do you mean?"

"Africans may marry two or three wives and build them separate houses. Neighbors, relatives, and friends know and respect that those are his wives. Such a man is too involved in keeping his family intact, in case the wives gang on him. Also, with too many eyes, polygamists have limited opportunity or energy to stray outside plural marriages."

"I still wonder how the women allow that to happen."

"You can ask the same question to the American women. Some married American men—like single-wife Africans, who are the majority, sneak around and get mistresses or indulge in one-nighters now and then. (I forgot to mention American serial marriages.) It all depends on whose style you want to malign—the polygamists' or the sneakers'—otherwise, it's two routes to the same multiple-partners' destination."

Mr. Insurance stirred, bit his lower lip, and snickered, but kept his lips sealed. He did not strike me as one who would mind the spoils of polygamy, maybe on the side with no responsibilities, the one-nighter type.

Chapter 9

Gone Forever

While I waited for the insurance settlement, Mr. Savior paid me a visit that changed everything. Money or no money, my return to Kenya became imminent.

He still lived on campus, on the fourth month of his doctoral program. Despite our relationship trailing off months earlier, I had kept my attacker abreast of my whereabouts. He was the only person I knew who could contact my family without language barrier if something happened to me.

Those were the telephone buggy days. Many people relied on pay phones and sometimes supplemented it with a messenger, not unlike in the days gone-by. In 1985, tech companies were in their infancy and had not introduced cell phones.

My family's messenger in Kenya paid a visit to my alma mater, USIU, Nairobi. The Student Affairs office there telexed my alma mater in San Diego. The Admissions Office in San Diego did not know where to find me; their records showed USIU as my last address. After contacting several African students, however, the

Office learned Mr. Savior had my contact information. They entrusted him with the delicate news.

His human side decided a phone call too impersonal. He drove from Scripps Ranch to Logan Heights. With GPS still to come, Mr. Savior got lost several times. He took over an hour to locate the address where I worked at Ms. Psychologist's house.

"I have bad news," he said. "Your mother passed away."

My life shattered. After I recovered somewhat from the shock, I said, "I'm so confused. What shall I do?" Actually, except feeling helpless, my mind had gone blank, frozen.

Mr. Savior stepped in, turned into a lean-on-me superman. "I'll make sure you get to Nairobi one way or the other," he said.

This refocused me. My mother, who had been my seven-year-old daughter's guardian in my absence, was stiff in a mortuary thousands of miles away in Nairobi. "How?" I asked. "I need at least $1000."

"I'll work on it. I'll have a fundraiser," he said.

Ms. Psychologist, my employer, sympathized and admired the Kenyan *Harambee*, let's-pull-together motto, when I told her of Mr. Savior's commitment. She could have afforded to kick in some money, but she kept her fists clenched. I hadn't shed the Kenyan expectation that, in times of need, everybody, family, friend, or stranger, should chip-in, although they sometimes did it begrudgingly.

Mr. Savior returned after three days—$1200 in hand. I asked him how he raised that much money in such a short time.

"I added $400 from my tuition money, but you need not bother yourself. Getting you to Nairobi is the important thing."

"I'll make sure you get your $400 when I get to Nairobi," I said, grateful most of the money was donation.

Air tickets were pricey at such a short notice, but with my unexpired student ID, Mr. Savior drove me to a travel agency that sold me a student discounted ticket on a British Airways flight for the exact amount he raised.

*

On the first leg of my journey, the flight to London, I sat next to an Indian man. It will be a nice quiet flight, I stereotyped. By the time we reached over the Atlantic Ocean, the Indian had proved me wrong. He had become chatty, uncharacteristic of what I knew of Indian men's attitude toward non-Indian women. He said he owned an Indian clothing store in New York. What is new? Up to that moment, the Indians I had met were shopkeepers or sons and daughters of shopkeepers. In Menengai High School in Kenya, where the Indians were the majority, African students believed Indians went to school to become better shopkeepers.

The man said he often went to India to buy merchandise. I wondered but resisted asking him why he boarded the British Airways flight in Los Angeles and not New York. We talked about various sari materials and Indian dressing.

Before we arrived at London's Heathrow Airport, the man invited me to accompany him to India, said it would be a trip of my life. I grinned, without a response. If it were today, I would be more forthcoming and tell him about the death in my family.

"When we arrive in London, I will buy you a round-trip ticket to India," he said. "I will pay for your one-week stay in India, and you don't worry about nothing. You return to London and go to Kenya."

"Thank you, but I would rather not."

He faced me, shook his head in slow motion as if surprised that an African woman refused such a generous offer from an Indian man. After a short pause, he offered me a future tour of his New York store.

"I doubt I will be back to America," I said.

We thereafter kept to ourselves.

*

My flight arrived at Heathrow airport in the morning. With a ten-hour layover, I had enough time to snoop around London and spend part of my $200 savings. Clothes at Marks and Spenser, and another store I do not remember, beckoned me since I visited London in 1977. To my detriment, I failed to change my watch to London time.

At the Immigration and Customs counter, the officer asked no more than three questions before he stamped a six-month residency visa in my Kenyan passport. Kenya, a former British colony, was still a respected member of the British Commonwealth.

And, Osama Bin Laden and company hadn't yet grown lethal tentacles that, in another sixteen years, would spook countries into guarding their borders vigilante style, just in case.

I boarded a train to downtown London. At one stop, a pin-striped-suited man, a gold band on his ring finger, boarded the train and sat next to me. I shifted in my seat to give him enough space and returned to my thoughts, sad face in place. "Where are you from?" startled me to a happier face. Before long he and I broached various topics about Kenya and England. I kept mum about America, thinking my experiences there could not make good conversation. My misery forgotten, I chatted on. When we arrived at the city center, the man asked if he could come along while I shopped. "Okay," I said. Perhaps he wanted to delay confronting a nag or two at home. Besides, company would keep my poor-me thoughts at bay.

We walked and talked and I shopped. To a casual observer, we looked like a modern African/European couple who cared for each other, strolling London streets having a good time. He helped me carry what I bought: skirt, sweater, slip, and a pair of shoes. While he walked me back to the train station, I asked him, "What would your wife think if she saw you accompany me like this?"

"What she doesn't know won't hurt her," he said in that sexy British accent.

I got on the Heathrow Airport train, smiled as I waved him goodbye, thankful for the interlude.

On my arrival at the airport, I found my flight to Nairobi had departed with my luggage on board. I took too long with Mr. Chummy and lost track of time. When my plane from Los Angeles arrived at Heathrow that morning, I had planned to change my watch to London time, but I ignored the nagging feeling I get when things are bound to go wrong.

I mentally stomped, kicked, and thought poorly of my judgment. My eyes teared and my vocal cords faltered when I spoke to the counter personnel. My trouble did not alter her professional stance. She repeated to clarify what I said or paused to give me time to say it clearer, and then rescheduled me for the next day's flight. I moved a few feet from the counter, stood to let my new reality sink in—twenty-four hours in which to wallow in my misery alone. A night at a London hotel was way beyond my budget. Minutes of self-pity and how low I felt on the human scale readied me to look around the airport lounge for a comfortable corner to hunker for the night.

Luckily, others hung around stranded like me, in the then damp looking, deserted waiting areas. Most of the people had marked their spots, like homeless people in front of locked stores and the main library doorways at night in downtown San Diego, supporting their heads or resting their legs on their luggage to discourage people with sticky hands. I marked my spot, three black chairs among the nailed-down rows, opposite a man seated alone—harder for a woman to be picked by a predator while next to a man. After I settled, I conversed with my neighbor, an Arab man—family type, white shirt no beard. Not the kind you befriend and when you disagree later comes to burn your house down while you are asleep. We talked, complained about the hard chairs, the cold night with nothing to cover with, and so forth. After the airport lights dimmed, we carried on our chatter until sleep overpowered the effect of the hard chairs.

When I awoke, it was morning. By late afternoon, I was on a Kenya Airways plane to Nairobi, a stewardess welcoming passengers aboard, first in Kiswahili then in English.

Chapter 10

Homecoming

When the captain announced to the crew to prepare for landing, expectant sensations oozed from every nerve ending in my body. In minutes, the plane touched down at Jomo Kenyatta International Airport. I am home! The sensations morphed into an overwhelming love—a buoyancy, almost orgasmic—followed by an indescribable sense of wellbeing—a-once-in-a-lifetime experience. I then understood why some people kneel to kiss the ground when they return to their homelands.

Like typical passengers, we hustled to get our carryon luggage from the overhead compartments or under our seats, and out the plane. Rush, rush to go wait in line at the customs. Foreigners ended in several long lines while I joined the citizens-only shorter line.

I found my luggage locked in with others that had gone astray or gone uncollected. I dragged it through the arrival lounge, littered by people who raised little boards bearing the names of people they came to meet. Others did not need boards—just eager faces. Lucky travelers to find people waiting for them. No one knew about my homecoming.

A taxi drove me through Airport Road and branched off into a shortcut through Outerring Road. It dropped me on Mutasi Court, Buru Buru Estate. The two-bedroom red-roof-tiled bungalow I bought in my twenties had been my home for the last eleven years; ten if you take out the year in America. There was no visible light or activity. That struck me as odd with death in the family. I expected to find my daughter, Mariana, the housekeeper, and a horde of mourners keeping vigil.

A lone streetlight at the cul-de-sac illuminated my way. What happened to the others? Dead bulbs? Inside the wooden gate, I stood for a minute, my eyes not yet adjusted. The wooden fence let minimal light into the yard. Halfway along the short driveway, I saw a light through the living room curtain crack, coming from the kitchen at the back. I knocked on the door. No homey noises, or sound of approaching steps—nothing. With my luggage next to me, worry embraced me, homecoming euphoria long gone. It was past midnight; my brother David's house was at least a mile away. The neighbors were already asleep.

I did not need to worry. The porch light came on.

Muriithi, my twenty-something brother, my parents' last-born by default, after Njomo, the actual last born, died at three, opened the door. He gasped, his eyes opened wide. "It's you!" he said. "I can't believe it! We were wondering whether you got the message."

"Yes, I got it."

"Oh, come in, come in." He stepped out to the porch without shoes, just his socks, reached for my big suitcase and hauled it inside. I followed him and placed my carryon luggage beside the TV in the living room. The three gold couches—a three-sitter and two one-sitters looked undisturbed, just like I left them a year ago, like time stopped when I left. Even the lacy white tablecloth on the six-chair dining table next to the green accent wall toward the kitchen hung slightly crooked just as it did before.

I walked by the coffee table and sat on the corner of the big couch across the TV.

"Where is everybody?" I asked.

"It's just me. Mariana is at David's," Muriithi said.

Just one week after my mother's death, the other occupants abandoned the house. The housekeeper returned to wherever she had come from. Word had reached me in America that she was like family. With her wage payer dead, she could not hold out for more than a week, not even for her pay for the two weeks she had already worked.

Mariana, at seven, felt the death the hardest. During the previous week, she had counted days, rushed home from school just in case doctors had discharged her grandmother. Instead, her grandmother had summoned her children to the hospital on the eve of her death. As a child, Mariana could not go due to hospital rules. A day later, Mariana learned her grandmother would not come home. She failed to understand "Never coming home." She did not want to live in that house anymore. The housekeeper walked her to her Uncle David's house to join her two cousins, two and three years her senior.

I found out the following day that well-wishers had turned out in droves at David's house. Availability of tea and bread and a wife to entertain the mourners helped.

As Muriithi updated me, I remained seated like a visitor, not interested in looking around the house I had not been in for a year. My mind went in all directions, unsure who I felt most sorry for—my dead mother in the mortuary, Mariana, or myself.

*

My mother suffered from poor health since I was a little girl. By the time I got out of school and bought a house in Nairobi, her sickness had escalated. She came to Nairobi to seek specialized treatment at Kenyatta National Hospital. During that period, she stayed in my house for two weeks to a month, got treatment, and returned to Solai. She still had my father and two minor children to look after.

When the children grew up and left the house, and my father died, Mother came to live with Mariana and me. She gradually helped turn my house into a home, and maintained it in my absence. When a year later I arrived from San Diego after her death, the same house felt cold and empty. Hardly the self-renewal I envisioned.

While in San Diego, I imagined how my mother would welcome me home—help to cook food to last us a week. How she would have spoiled me, bombarded me with questions about America, and bragged about me to her friends. All my tribulations while in America would have seemed trivial and worth it.

With her gone, and my father's death five years earlier, I felt orphaned—a grown-up orphan—wandering all alone in a psychological wilderness.

*

By Christmas of 1985, two months had gone by since I arrived from the USA. Mariana and I huddled on the three-sitter couch. The house felt empty. We had never spent a holiday just the two of us. In my quest to fill the void, and for Mariana's sake, I put up a Christmas tree. No relief—I remained miserable. Mariana acted happy although she tugged on me everywhere, in case I disappeared again.

I had no a clue how our lives would go on. Usually, I have a rough projection of about a year, but at that time I hadn't factored in my mother's death. It never occurred to me she would die in my absence. Sickness was part of her life. In between doctor visits, she had toiled for her children and did whatever she needed to do to see them grow and go to school.

My mother must have been waiting for my return because she did not last two months after she received the graduation photo I sent to her. She paraded the passport-size shot to friends, family, and her church group. I felt guilty for not sending her a bigger picture and for my inability to return home before she died, let alone the mother-daughter sharing opportunity lost.

It touched my heart even more to discover how she valued the photo. She kept it among five 100-shilling notes and a cassette recording of her will, stashed in a pouch at the bottom corner of her trunk she kept in the bedroom she shared with Mariana. She allowed no one to sleep in my bedroom, kept it under lock and key so no one could sneak in and disturb my belongings.

All that care counted for nothing to me. Except Mariana returning to school, I never cared or saw beyond a month. The nuclear family—Mother, Mariana, a woman to help us around the house, and I—was the only family Mariana had known, except unannounced family members' comings and goings.

A father for her and a partner for me would have come in handy.

*

My mind flashed back to one evening when Mariana was four. She returned to the house at dusk after her play with the neighborhood children at the cul-de-sac. I sat on my usual spot on the big couch, my mother on the opposite single-sitter. Mariana plopped her little body next to mine. She cocked her head to look up at me, and asked in Kiswahili, "How come we don't have a father?" I suspected her playmates had put ideas in her head, or she was old enough to notice the void in our household.

My mother threw me a knowing glance, her lips zipped. I knew that look. A fellow she thought would make a perfect son-in-law and great husband for me went bye-bye. My mother failed to understand when I said the relationship fell through. Her stepfather coerced her to marry my father, so my fell-through claim eluded her.

I let my mother be, doubtful she and I would see the intricacies of a relationship the same way. But I needed to answer Mariana's question. My brain indulged me with thoughts that crystalized into pristine clarity without plan or effort on my part. Using examples of our neighbors' family structures, I explained our fatherless state. I told her about the "father-only" household on the right side of our house. I hoped she had not noticed the girlfriend who came every weekend to visit the man and that there was no child, and call me on it. She did not. I said ours was a mother-only family. I omitted to ask her whether she preferred the present set-up, or to have my bones broken by a drunk for her to have a father. Next, I pointed out the family on our left, a mother and a teacher by day, her office-worker husband, and four children. After I finished, Mariana paused—possibly looking for holes in my explanation. She said, "Aaaaah!" The subject never came up again.

*

Mourning proved a big challenge. I had witnessed four other deaths in my family before—two brothers, my father, and an aunt—but none had hit me as hard as my mother's. I reminisced about my past, nothing about the future. My head and body did not act right. I felt lethargic and drew blanks in my thinking. When I walked, sometimes I suffered a one-second blackout, missed a step and swayed. Other times I tripped. I diagnosed myself: Depression. Oh my, why did I think going away could rejuvenate me? I am even worse. Please, please, it is bad to think that way. Or it could be something else—a brain tumor?

To add to my misery, I received a $600 demand letter from Kathy all the way in San Diego. According to her letter, Mr. Savior borrowed the amount from her for me. This was unknown to me. I recalled when I asked Mr. Savior about "fundraising" money that fast, he made me believe in his popularity and ability when he cocked his head one side and gave me a satisfied look. Kathy's claim sounded authentic. She did not know my Kenyan address and could have got it only from Mr. Savior. I had no money to send to her or the fortitude to write and explain. I ignored her letter.

*

As I fumbled through my miserable life, an ex-boyfriend informed me that the government gave jobs to college graduates returning from overseas. He urged me to apply. I knew of such practice before I left the country.

From when Kenya attained its independence on December 12, 1963 to the 1970s, the government rushed to train its citizens to occupy posts formerly held by the British colonialists. University graduates educated abroad, especially in specialized fields like engineering and medicine, were an added boost to the program. The government paid their way back to Kenya, where the graduates found waiting jobs. In doing so, the government followed a degree pecking order. Eastern European degree holders received no or minimal attention. Those from the United States had a better standing, but Kenyans considered them a tad lower than the ones from the University of Nairobi, or Makerere University in Uganda. The Harvards and the Yales toiled under the radar, except to the few well-travelled. Degree holders from Britain, in particular Oxford and Cambridge, came at the top of the heap.

After about a decade of this inflow, the enticement packages—free transportation and specific waiting jobs—got slimmer and slimmer. Some graduates started settling in whatever country they trained. Kenya politicians and other officials worried about brain drain. But by 1986 whispers abounded that the recruiting exercise had turned into a face-saving gimmick. That there were no jobs to go around, despite politicians' claim that "Our government can take care of its own people." The officials offered these eager arrivals only paper-pushing entry positions, glorified messengers of sorts.

The government did not need to worry about me—I was not looking for a job. I lacked the strength to attend any office interview, or the desire to push any papers. Instead of a job, I first needed therapy, a new concept I picked up in America. But, if I disclosed it to my do-gooder friends and family, they would have laughed it off, credited it to American indoctrination. Therapy to them was for mentally ill people, not regulars like me. If people had problems, they discussed them with their friends.

Only one idea kept popping in my fuzzy thinking—to return to the United States. Not because of a longing or need to be in America, but our house felt like an empty shell. In my mental state, I was of no benefit to Mariana or to myself. I needed to lose—or find—myself by living somewhere else. But where? Nowhere could I have gone in Kenya for total separation. In San Diego, I was broke, alone, and miserable, my body and mind in a strained state, but my head never drew blanks. Even if I had, I would have likely blamed it on American unfriendliness toward immigrants and black people— real and imagined, picked from immigrants' rampant hush-hush exchanges.

I liquidated a two-acre plot I owned in Ongata Rongai, in the outskirts of Nairobi, which I had designated as financial backup to pay expenses while I looked for a job when I returned home. With my life upside down, I re-budgeted the money. I used some of it to buy an open one-way British Airways ticket to San Diego. But, I still had Mariana's welfare to think about.

First, I could hardly support myself, let alone both of us, in San Diego. Even if I could, there was no way the American Embassy, with its stringent requirements, would have issued her an entry visa. I therefore arranged for her to live with my sister's family in Thika until I sorted myself psychologically. Meanwhile, I obtained a passport for her to quicken the visa process when the time came for her to travel.

*

My travel plans remained known to close confidants only, but somehow my family sniffed the news miles away.

While Mariana and I watched TV one evening, we heard a knock on the door. It was my brother Simon from Solai, 120 miles away, with no jacket and only a tiny overnight bag in hand. Why? Why? I had no energy to entertain. We exchanged greetings. He gave Mariana two packets of biscuits he brought for her—a small consolation. Besides compassion, generosity was another remarkable thing about my brother. Unlike other men in my family, he always brought a token gift, especially if there was a child in the home.

While he drank tea and ate the food I offered him, he updated me on the village gossip and other family matters. Nobody was sick or dead, the rain had come, the crops were thriving, and the children were in school. "*Notwiyumiriirie*, we are still hanging on," he said. That tiring, stifling Gikuyu term I wished they would retire, already.

I wished I could ask him, *why are you here then?*

I cleared the kitchen, and we watched the last movie; TVs programs ended at 11:00 p.m. back then. After the movie, I deposited a pillow, blanket and a pair of sheets on the three-sitter couch for him. I joined Mariana in my bedroom.

The next morning after breakfast, Simon said, "*Ndiraigua ndumiriri ati niurenda gucoka* America. *Uhoro ucio uthinitie ngoro muno*, I have heard news you want to return to America. I'm very concerned by the news."

"Ummmm…," I said.

"I came to speak to you and confirm whether this is true or just a rumor."

I hesitated.

"So it's true?" he said, without waiting for my answer. "I beg you not to return to that place. It's just too far. I promise the family will not bother or make demands on you."

How did he know about my complaints? Perhaps Mother had spread the word in her quest to shield me from relatives. Simon begged me. I promised him, lied, that I would think about it.

If I had any doubts about returning to America, Simon's coming to my house unannounced doubled my resolve. Flashbacks of the burden my family had placed on me flooded my mind. Pre-urbanization, people expected unannounced drop-ins. But with population moving into cities where people bought food—not cultivated it—things changed. Even in rural areas, the practice was not always welcome, unless one dropped in bearing gifts that outweighed the inconvenience and did not expect return bus fare.

Yes, I would go back to America. For how long?—I had not thought that far.

*

For a visa to reenter United States of America, I needed proof of support. I looked around for people who owed me from my past. A politician, through his construction company in my hometown, Nakuru, agreed to fund my education that time around. After checking the construction company's financial records, and my school readmission papers, the American Embassy in Nairobi issued me a re-entry visa.

The on-again off-again politician in charge would later renege on the promise after I returned to San Diego. He also liquidated and spent my money from an eight-acre plot he held in trust and as collateral. I must admit, however, that he, with his phantom financial backing was, in part, instrumental in my returning to the United State in 1986.

With travel arrangements in place, I went to the British Airways' office and scheduled a flight to San Diego.

*

Nineteen months earlier, when I first traveled to America, I had a multitude of people—I heard at least forty—escort me to the airport. But the second time, it was only my sister Wairimu and a friend. After they dropped me off, they had to go somewhere else before they returned to the house in Buru Buru. So, they didn't want Mariana to join them. That mistake gnaws on my mind whenever I remember the monstrous tantrum she threw and her pleas that I not return to America without her.

Mariana knew I had obtained a passport for her, which I explained was for when the American government said she could go.

It failed to pacify her. I doubt she will ever forgive me, at least for not letting her escort me to the airport.

Chapter 11

Miss Nutcase

I returned to San Diego and reported to USIU in mid-1986. I sought help from the two people who still passed for my friends—Ms. Psychologist, whose boys I babysat the year before, and Mr. Savior, my abusive ex-boyfriend. He allowed me to sneak behind school officials and spend a week at his apartment on campus, eating food purchased from Von's Supermarket. Ms. Psychologist embarked on searching for an off-campus accommodation for me. In my mind, I had outgrown babysitting and, better still, she viewed me as a friend, not as a potential employee.

A woman she knew needed a live-in assistant who could type and file. With my extensive secretarial training in Kenya, it sounded like a great opportunity for both the prospective employer and me. Ms. Psychologist drove me to the job interview that turned out to be just a formality. The two women had already agreed on my employment.

My new employer lived in Point Loma in a two-story, two-bedroom townhouse—bedrooms upstairs and kitchen, dining area, living room, and a two-car garage downstairs. She employed me to do minor housework—dusting and washing dishes. But she mainly wanted me to file, type, and establish a filing system for her files. In exchange, she offered me accommodation and $100 per month. I would provide for my meals.

The woman worked for the San Diego County or the City of San Diego, I forget which. She brought no work home. Her filing system involved files in a small two-drawer cabinet. Maybe she needed company. When I mentioned about the little work, she rushed upstairs saying, "Come, I'll show you how I want the files done."

"I've already done them," I said, following behind her.

She rolled the one-cart drawer closer to her recliner, sat, and fingered the file-folders.

I explained the filing system I used.

"Well, if you don't think you've enough to do, you could look for another part-time job during your school breaks."

Before long, I noticed the woman, without her public mask, flashy clothing, and high-strung air of importance, had a nutty side. Her townhouse was no place for me to nurse settling-down ideas. She slept in her recliner in her bedroom so as not to disturb her bed. We did not eat at the dining table—it stayed laid-out with fine china, napkins in glasses, like in a showroom. The kitchen counter served our dining needs, which was just coffee for her. Every part of her townhouse, including herself, was a showcase. At about five-foot-ten, her attractive clothes flowed down her slim body, model-like. If only she could discard the over-size earrings she sometimes wore, similar to the hideous gaudy ones some black women insist on wearing.

My other unspecified duty was to accompany her to dinner—she never cooked—on the rare occasion she had not eaten before she came home, or when she did not have other company. She also dragged me along to the few social events she attended. Once we arrived at an event, she walked around, smile in place, eager to introduce me, "Meet my assistant…." My body recoiled. I preferred the assistant angle remain undisclosed, just between us. The negligible work I did for her gave hardworking assistants a bad name. It must have boosted her public image; I saw guests throw her envious glances. Who knew what demons she had to slay on her way to adulthood and to managerial status? I did not breathe a word about my demons or that I boomeranged to college to escape that assistant business. Assistant or secretary—I didn't know the difference—shuffling in and out of a boss's office, pen and pad on the ready, and day-in, day-out guard duty—was what I longed to avoid.

*

"Miss Nutcase" had a friend who had no business wearing his signature dreary suit. His tightened belt made his trousers gather as if it were one size bigger. She introduced him as a sex therapist. That sounded weird to a confirmed prude like me; I had never heard of the term. Who needed a therapist to get rid of a horny situation? The two talked like it was a respectable profession, saying everybody needed such therapy before marriage.

One evening, Dr. Therapist dropped in before Miss Nutcase returned home. He and I conversed as acquaintances. Men are easy to get along with, if you ask me. In a moment of self-serving, I let it slip that my days at the townhouse were limited.

"I understand," he said, nodding slowly.

See what I mean? Men are such team players. They do not need an hour's gossipy explanation before they are onboard.

How did he understand? I did not ask.

In another month, Miss Nutcase and I could not live together without clawing each other's eyes out. I do not recall the reasons, but it was mutual. We called it quits one Friday evening. She told me to clear out of her house the following day. She would pay me the $60— $10 of which she had borrowed when she didn't have cash on her— that I had coming, after my belongings were out the front door. At that stage, she irritated me so much I did not care if she threw me into the streets that very night. I had prepared Ms. Psychologist for such an eventuality. I called her. She had to facilitate a group workshop the whole of Saturday. We agreed I call her late afternoon. I turned to the only other person who could help me move—Dr. Therapist.

Saturday morning, I packed my effects and got them by the main door, ready for the afternoon move. In the process of hauling my suitcase from the bedroom upstairs, I accidentally (Miss Nutcase said "intentionally") poked a hole with a corner of my suitcase in a giant clay vase that stood by the stairwell. If you ever get a chance, try living in a showcase residence without breaking something—can't do it.

To replace or repair the vase, Miss Nutcase withheld the sixty dollars she owed me.

The loss ticked me off so much that I thought of sticking my tongue at her while I got moved by none other than her sex-therapist friend. Too childish an act. Instead, I threw mental darts at her and wished bad karma would lend me a hand. It bothered me constantly before passage of time diluted the grudge, no matter how much I nursed and hung onto it.

Miss Nutcase, disgusted that Dr. Therapist volunteered to move me, left so as not to bear witness while he helped me load my belongings into his car. I told him about Ms. Psychologist coming for me later. I did not know how to direct him to her house in Logan Heights. I had no key to her house, anyway.

"No problem. You can come and wait in my house," Dr. Therapist said.

We passed through his office—three offices with a common waiting room. He introduced me to another therapist who asked me questions about Africa using terms like *motherland,* which I thought suspect when asked by a white man. The man looked like the few people I had met whom I later learned people referred to as "black," yet looked white. Apparently, in America, you could call a white-looking person—pink, blue eyes, the whole package—black but never, ever think or call a white-looking 'black' person white.

We left the office and arrived at Dr. Therapist's L-shaped house early evening. What neighborhood, I could not tell you. The house was cool with an unlived-in quietness. He switched on a table light and turned on an old TV. News or sports came on. It gave the house life. Did we have dinner? I do not recall. The one clear thing is that I felt no hunger pangs, but I wished he could offer me a cup of tea.

I called Ms. Psychologist at around 8:00 p.m. She was still in her office. Dr. Therapist and I had already concluded it was tiring for her to drive at night from Bonita, about seven miles away. We agreed she come for me the following day.

At about 9:00 p.m., Dr. Therapist said, "I'll show you the bedroom." He took my suitcase from where he set it down by the living room wall. I followed him. A whiff of stale sweaty odor assaulted my nose the minute I entered.

"My daughters' room," he said. "They come weekends, but they went elsewhere this weekend. You can use it for a few days if you like."

"Thank you for letting me sleep here tonight." I glanced from one bed to the other.

"You can pick either bed."

The twin beds were parallel, about six feet apart, each with a dresser at the foot. The bedding had seen better days, and the beds slightly sagged in the middle.

I went to the bathroom to prepare for bed—the bare basics–washed my face and brushed my teeth.

I chose the sturdier looking of the two beds. Since I wanted to leave my suitcase undisturbed, I removed the sweater I wore and got in between the sheets fully clothed. As I drew the covers to my neck, I stopped, held my breath midstream, and then exhaled slowly. The smell intensified in the bed. Awful! Instead of taking another breathe I sprang up.

I straightened the sheets and cover over the bed, took my handbag and returned to the living room. I sat down on the old couch, where I sat before. I could breathe again, but I agonized on what to tell Dr. Therapist. Before a sound answer came to mind, he appeared from his bedroom.

"Are you okay?"

Two years in the United States and already tired of the question—Are you okay? Couldn't people reserve it for benign upsets—mine qualified, I suppose. But no. Someone drops half-dead or cries buckets and the first question to hear is "Are you okay?"

I wanted to tell the man, "Of course I'm not okay! Can't breathe in a bed that smells like a hair chemical cesspool!"—a hypocritical outburst by a person who frowned at certain entitlements. Instead, I said, "I'm fine."

"Don't you want to sleep in the bedroom?"

"It makes me uncomfortable to be in there without your daughters' permission."

"They won't mind."

"I would rather sleep on the couch, if it's all right with you."

"Fair enough." He re-entered his bedroom and returned clutching a comforter in one hand and dangling a pillow in the other. "Lemme know if you need anything else."

"Thank you."

Yes, the couch felt much better and firmer. I returned to thoughts of my instability and imminent homelessness—how my life would unravel in this unexpected America, a juggernaut full of twists and turns, unappalled human tapestry, misery and glamor, music and dance, hopes and dreams galore.

Dr. Therapist interrupted my thoughts when he poked his head out of his bedroom door again. That time to inform me sleeping on the couch was uncomfortable.

I kept quiet about the *revelation*.

"You are welcome to share my bed," he said.

It never fails.

Chapter 12

Roommates and Apartment

When Ms. Psychologist let me into her home in Logan Heights, we did not discuss the conditions or the length of my stay. But I resolved to find an alternative residence in a hurry to minimize self-generated stress by becoming too cautious not to infringe on the family's routine and comfort.

When I look back, however, my presence caused minimal disruption because she and her children ate most of their meals outside the home. I ate a hamburger at a fast-food restaurant or at my favorite Chinese buffet by Fourth and Broadway, downtown San Diego. I did this after I scouted for want-ad signs placed on windows or live-in positions posted at the library, at that time situated on E Street between Seventh and Eighth Streets. I also checked in newspapers for rooms for rent.

On the third day at Ms. Psychologist's, I read an ad for a $200-per-month room in a two-bedroom apartment in Normal Heights. Sonny answered the phone when I called. He confirmed the amount of rent and said we would split the electric bill half-and-half.

He said to take bus number eleven and get off on Adams' Avenue and 34th Street, about four miles from Logan Heights.

In about an hour, I travelled in a bus seated in one of the front seats, opposite the driver's side. When I estimated we had covered the four miles, I leaned toward the driver, "Can you please let me know when I get to 34th Street and Adams Avenue?"

"Lady, your stop is on the other end—that way." He pointed north-west.

"What do I do now?" then on my feet, all rattled, one hand clutching my bag's straps onto the seat frame, the other hanging on to the overhead bus rail to steady myself.

"Not to worry. I'll get there eventually. Or you can wait for another bus across the street."

I got off at the next bus stop.

*

The apartment occupied part of the ground floor of a two-story building, yards south of Adams Avenue. A Middle-Eastern man answered my knock. Another one sat at the dining table by the kitchen counter. Oh, my! Share an apartment with two Arab men. *At least they don't have the scary beards.*

"I'm Sonny. Come in." He shook my hand. "I'm the one who talked to you on the phone." Sonny, medium build and height, said they were Iranians. He introduced his skinnier older brother, then added, "My girlfriend is the other roommate."

I relaxed, but hoped she did not wear the signature black floor-sweeping shapeless gowns with head-wraps or drapes.

Sonny showed me the empty room with overused but clean sage-green carpet. With little conversation between us, I checked for scratches and nicks, rolled the wall-to-wall closet doors both ways, checked the window latch, and said, "I'll take it," similar to what I saw tenants do on TV programs, mistakenly believing in America landlords accepted every tenant who liked their rental property. It worked for me that time, though. I paid Sonny the $200 in cash. The amount covered the bedroom and shared kitchen, living room, and bathroom. I would pay half of the electric bill. Except what I told Sonny on the phone, that I was a student and did temporary jobs, he asked me no other details, not even a security deposit.

Ms. Psychologist helped me move. Evening arrived by the time she left me to settle in my new quarters. It had been a long productive day. I closed the bedroom door and indulged in a burst of brief hand and leg moves to celebrate my first rental in America.

After I freshened, I tackled my belongings—a box and bag of books, a carry-on, and my big suitcase. When I hung most of my clothes, the suitcase still held two wrappers, one half-size blanket from a garage sale in college, and one brown blanket I bought at Kmart when I first arrived in San Diego two years earlier. I had left the items at Ms. Psychologist's house when I went to my mother's funeral. It did not cross my mind, or I felt embarrassed to ask her to give me bedding from the heaps strewn all over her enclosed patio.

Or I wanted to live light until I stopped relying on other people to move me.

Anyway, for the night, I spread the half blanket on the carpet as bedding, rolled one wrapper into a pillow, and used the other wrapper and Kmart blanket as cover. Despite the hardness of the concrete, my mind settled, and I fell into deep sleep.

*

Within the week, I noticed "head of household" was Sonny's fulltime job. He slept most of the day. Once he emerged from the bedroom, he groomed himself, paying particular attention to his face and hair. He then waited for his Latina girlfriend to come from her City or County job. Whenever she arrived home, he asked what she planned to cook for dinner. If he did not like her answer, he voiced his preference, and she made a switch. After they ate, mostly chicken and rice, they retired to their bedroom where TV remained on until the wee hours of morning. The dirty dishes, and pots and pans remained in the sink until she came home the following day.

On the other hand, Sonny's brother was an uptight, pious, twenty-something who walked with his shoulders hunched. He slept on the floor in one corner of the living room. Farther down lay his prayer mat that he used five times daily. He lamented about his younger brother's laziness and fornication. But from the look of the household setup, the woman sinner may have been their sole provider.

"Mr. Pious" claimed he went to school. I saw sporadic absences, praying, and reading Islamic books, with an occasional heated quarrel with his brother in Arabic. I ignored him, unaware a decade and a half later, I, and many other Americans, would be wary of a person with similar mannerisms.

In two months, I felt tired.

Tired of sleeping on the floor and waking with body aches like an old woman,

Tired and irritated by Miss Latina's lack of backbone,

Tired of Mr. Pious' prayers and complaints,

Tired of riding two buses to college, and getting home after 11:00 p.m.,

Tired of hunting all over San Diego for part-time jobs,

Tired of Sonny's shallowness and his noisy all-night TV racket.

And, I felt tired of his cheating. Four people lived in that apartment, but I paid half the electric bill. I paid half of the first bill, which arrived barely two weeks after I moved in. When the second bill came, it sounded too high. I asked to see the bill three times before Sonny showed it to me. The amount included the previous bill although I had given him the money. I called him on it. He complained about the electric company's inefficiency, that they had failed to credit his payment.

Above all, I felt tired of living on survival mode, groping through an invisible maze without a clue on how to get out. I surrendered, drifted along—and waited for something, anything, to come up.

Something did come up all right. When I returned home one evening, Mr. Pious said, "A man called you. His number is on the dining table."

"A man?" I asked, on my way to my bedroom, not in the least interested.

"Yes."

"What did he want?"

"I thought it was a crank call and almost hung up on him."

Although about to enter my bedroom, to be civil, I waited for him to finish talking.

"But he said his insurance company owes you money. Did you work for them?"

"No." Then my memory rushed in, I stopped, turned around, bag of books still in hand, headed to the dining table. I picked the little piece of paper, looked at the number to ensure Mr. Pious had not missed a digit.

"Do you know him?"

"Not really," I said, paper gripped in my palm.

"Call him anyway. He could be legit."

"I will. Thank you."

In my room, I closed the door, something I did only when dressing or going to sleep. After I put down my bag of books, I stood still; shut my eyes as relief swept through me while I clenched the tiny paper in both hands to my chest, breathing steadily.

I had forgotten the previous year's bus accident on La Jolla Village Drive. The shock of my mother's death had not only wiped it from my mind, but also made me ignore and forget achy muscles and over-stretched ligaments. Without attention, my body quit complaining. The insurance company still owed me the $800 they promised. How did they track me down?

My outlook on life brightened in a flash. *Money can't buy happiness.* Go tell that to someone else. A shopping list formed in my mind. In the 1980s, $800 could buy me the basic comforts I craved and freedom from Mr. Sonny and his cohorts. I tucked the phone number in my wallet and wished morning to hurry.

I called the insurance man at 9:00 a.m. He said they had looked for me for a year and that his company still held my $1,500 accident settlement.

"I thought it was $800," I said. Did I haggle to stick to the budget my mind had compiled? No. I just did not want to get disappointed when the man realized his mistake.

"It was, but the company decided to award you $1,500."

Perhaps they mistook my disappearance as a settlement rebuff in favor of a lawsuit and threw in the extra $700 to coax the thorny issue away. Whatever the reason, luck had appeared to bail me yet again.

In two days, a representative—not sure whether it was the same Mr. Insurance who interviewed me before, I couldn't tell the difference—came to the apartment. He suggested we sit at the dining table. From his briefcase, he took out stacks of paperwork and a check for $1,500, in my name.

"I need you to sign these papers." He gave me one stack to sign and another for my records. He hung on to the check. He said, "By signing and accepting the $ 1,500 check, you are confirming you have no further claim against...insurance company...."

I reached for the pen he had put on the table.

"You should read before you sign," he said.

I signed the pile of papers without reading. Mr. Pious, done with his day's second prayer, witnessed my signature.

Check in hand, I boarded bus number eleven through Hillcrest to downtown, went to my bank and deposited the windfall. I splurged on a $3.50 Chinese buffet to celebrate and to put in writing the list that had formed in my head the previous evening.

In days, I landed a furnished studio apartment in downtown. The manager quoted me a monthly rent of $275 with $150 security deposit. I haggled he lower the amount to $250.

"I've heard no one haggle on rent before," the manager said.

"You'll never say that again," I said.

"I'll ask the landlord and let you know."

In about three days, he called and told me the owner had agreed to $265.

After I signed the rental agreement, I gave Sonny a two-week notice to move. We, he and I, were not privy to a 30-day notice legal requirement.

*

My studio apartment was on the ground floor of an old walk-up four-story building on Front Street, between Beech and Cedar Streets. The steps to the roomy porch led straight to a double-door glass entrance. One could see the hallway to the ground floor and stairwell to the upper apartments. A regular glass-door on the right, with a white cloth curtain gathered at the top and bottom, led to my studio. The studio's two exterior walls had huge windows—one of its best features—and cream drapes. If I opened the drapes the light flooded in, and the studio looked like a huge veranda. The furnishings were typical: two couches, end tables, a coffee table, and a four-chair dining table just outside the kitchen, which curved in out of view from the front door. The kitchen had a gas stove, and an ancient sturdy refrigerator. An assortment of dishes and pots in the cupboard had seen better days. A pullout full-size bed pushed into a hollow area between the kitchen and the big closet, next to the bathroom.

It was exhilarating to call the phone company to connect my first phone in America. I treated myself to an answering machine and a used fifteen-dollar thirteen-inch black-and-white TV. I felt like a normal human being again. During the day when I had no temp job to go to, I watched soaps and talk shows on my very own TV.

Chapter 13

Free Rides

In my quest to break into American society, it seemed wherever I went men were the majority—down-on-their-luck men, scruffy men, sly men—all sorts of men. Take my apartment building for instance: I had not seen women or office-type residents. Most of the men there looked underfed and scruffy, except the manager who seemed overfed and an African-American/Mexican couple down the hall. I had no idea white people could look so beat-up by life like the people I looked at with distrust in Nairobi.

I hungered for human interaction and sometimes chitchatted with the manager. One day he took me into his confidence. "Some of these tenants need to stay in rehab," he said. The majority stayed clean, but might have suffered permanent damage. He fell off the wagon, he said, but worked on himself and got back on. It appeared he replaced his drug habit with food. He shuffled, toes facing outward, after parking his ancient Ford or Chevy, his grocery bags weighing him down on both sides. Within months, he lost his job or quit and became a regular tenant. Years later, I found out excessive eating could qualify a person for a government check, similar to a monthly salary—another Unexpected America. I do not know whether my ex-manager qualified for such a check, but afterward he ate and watched TV in peace, without tenants disturbing him.

Another chatty, scruffy drug survivor became the new manager.

*

The men I met in the larger population varied. Two weeks hardly passed before I witnessed benign or potential mini drama. The worst I had experienced, so far, was an occasional bus rider having a bad day and mouthing off to a fellow rider. If everyone ignored the troublemaker, lack of an audience calmed him. Once I gathered courage and made a comment. My non-American accent produced the same effect, even extracted a questioning look.

Sometimes ignoring a rider or a different accent had no effect on some people. Such was the case one afternoon when I kept company of a man of about twenty with uncombed hair, curled in little balls, wearing uncared-for dirty clothes. He stood about twenty-five feet away at a bus stop in Hillcrest, near UCSD Hospital. The bus stop had no bench or canopy, just a post that listed several bus route numbers. I threw the man an occasional cursory look, but his presence did not bother me; three other people stood by waiting for their buses.

A bus stopped about ten feet from me. The three people hurried and entered the bus. The young man followed. He stood on the doorstep, held onto the frame with his left hand and handed over his bus ticket to the driver. The driver told him, in not-so-subtle words, that the bus ticket was yesterday's. "What? Yesterday's?" the man asked. He took the expired ticket from the driver and examined it. He then threw his hand up, mumbled something and stepped down to the curb, stroking the ticket between his index finger and thumb. The bus left; the man returned where he stood before. It was then he and I. I looked straight ahead, uneasy, but pretended I did not notice his exchange with the bus driver.

We both waited, I for my bus, but I wondered what he waited for; his bus had turned him down. After about five minutes, I watched from the corner of my eye as he gingerly walked toward me. When he got near, I turned, noticed his red eyes and a body that seemed to have known a good home before but now ruled by a substance it could not handle.

My mind and heart cowed, but I willed my eyes to watch him as I would any other person approaching me.

"Hello," I said, using my mantra when I happen by iffy-looking people, to gauge the height of their hostility, if any.

"May I have a dollar?" he asked. His fingers still massaged his rejected yesterday's bus ticket, perhaps to show me as evidence.

"I'm sorry, I don't have a dollar," I said with a leave-me-alone finality.

"I just want a dollar."

"I don't have it."

He reverted to his non-verbal skills. He assumed a hangdog look and lazily focused his red eyes on me for seconds, then shifted his eyes to my handbag that I hugged under my armpit, then back to my eyes. Before his eyes moved to my bag a second time, I got the message.

I opened my handbag, took out a dollar, and surrendered it to him.

"Thank you," he said and returned to his spot. I left him there when my bus arrived.

*

Other drama came from drivers who stopped to offer me rides. With a twenty-mile bus ride, which took about two hours to meander through Pacific Beach, La Jolla, Mira Mesa, and into Scripps Ranch, I welcomed such offers, although a few times I declined when drivers looked too anxious I get in their cars. In cases like those, I lied that I was waiting for my ride. In my mind, however, it was like Nairobi of my days—a help-your-fellow-human-being kind of deal. Most men had other ideas. Twice, two different men drove into a secluded area and begged for massages, or wanted to masturbate while I watched. Both times an abrupt separation ensued and, instead of a free ride, I missed my bus, and had to wait for an hour before another one came.

After the two incidents, I became vigilant in my selection of the men from whom to accept rides—executive-type only. Not long after, one afternoon, an expensive-looking car, like the one my ex-friend, Mr. Millionaire, drove down in Florida, slowed down and stopped feet from where I stood waiting for my bus on First Avenue and Ash. The man opened the passenger window and shouted, "Do you need a ride?"

I hurried to the car and leaned close to the open window.

"What's a beautiful woman doing at a bus stop?"

I smiled.

"Where are you going?"

"I'm going to school…it's in Scripps Ranch."

"That's a long way. Come on in." He pressed the control by his door so I could turn the door handle.

I got in, made myself comfortable while he pulled back onto First Street.

Wow! What a car. Maroon in color—my favorite—and it had the rich-look the working class can only fantasize about.

People driving expensive-looking cars impressed me before I realized some of the cars were just a façade. Sorry, I meant net worth—a show-off car instead of a healthy bank account or an investment. Even today, it's not unusual to see a person drive a sleek Beamer or a Benz only to park it in front of an apartment building or a house mortgaged to the hilt—pay the rent or mortgage late, too.

The ride offers came before I learned of the façade. That is why the maroon car enamored me. While I feasted my eyes, the man drove over I-5 south freeway overpass, missed the entrance to route 163 Freeway to USIU. He continued on First Avenue headed north.

I did not fret. Perhaps he preferred to get to Sixth Avenue and catch 163 farther north.

"You must be a big executive to afford this kind of car," I said.

"Yes," he did not expound, but instead asked, "Why do you stay so far from school?"

"It's where I found an affordable apartment, and it's close to transportation," I said. "What do you do?"

"I produce a magazine in Los Angeles." He cocked his thumb toward the back seat.

"Oh," I turned my head; the bulky magazine looked unfamiliar. It did not occur to me to wonder how he knew I lived far from school if he came from Los Angeles.

"I'm here on business. I've just come from a meeting, and I'm going back to my hotel to relax."

"It's very nice of you to offer me a ride."

He paused. "Does money excite you?"

What a stupid question? Who does not like money? "Not for the sake of it. What do you mean?" I asked.

"The question is: Does money excite you?"

Is he challenging my intelligence? He looked like someone who could give me a job later on. "Money excites me, especially when I do something well, get recognized, and paid for it. I get such a sense of accomplishment." That ought to show him I have sense.

"Money…doesn't…excite you?" He said—not to me—to himself as he nodded.

We were then in the middle of Banker's Hill.

Mr. Magazine slowed the car and pulled at a bus stop, pointed at it and said, "That's your bus stop…that's where you belong."

I turned and faced him with a questioning look.

"Go on, go on," he said, waving me out with his backhand.

I stepped on the curb before my brain sorted his reaction. I leaned on the bus stop sign. What was that about? Oh…*that*'s what he wanted.

*

The one car I hesitated about, the minute it stopped at the First Avenue bus stop, turned out the charm. The driver wore a navy-blue outfit, like a coverall, with an awful crown of oily curls down to his neck. When I concluded he was harmless and got in his car, he said, "If a sister want education, I'll take her wherever she can get some." We had a smooth drive all the way to Scripps Ranch. Before we arrived, the distance weighed on his generosity. "It sure is far." I doubted he had ventured that far before. Nonetheless, when we arrived, he wore a satisfied grin when I thanked him and implied he had contributed to university education.

*

Accepting rides from strangers sounds dangerous and irresponsible. But it is all a matter of perspective. I never thumbed for a ride; the drivers stopped on their own accord. And up to that time, I remained ignorant of hitchhikers' kidnappings or others ending in shallow graves.

Besides, when I was growing up in Solai, no one had a car. It was a treat and a rare occasion when we rode a bus to Nakuru town, twenty miles away. We feasted our eyes on the town's cars during such visits, but never thought much about them—it was not our world. The only other moving vehicle we rode in was a tractor-drawn wagon owned by my parents' employer, which I doubt I rode in over three times, if that.

The closest I came to a car was the early sixties, the day our neighbor Alan's son-in-law, Mr. Mbuthia, bought one. He shelled a whopping 500 shillings ($5 in today's money) and drove the clunker home for its first and last drive. Words of excitement swept through the village from the mouths of the children, the women, and the men alike. I saw the car in his yard, raised on four stone blocks, chickens taking refuge from the sun in daytime. I could not understand why he bought the car and not drive it until I overheard grownups repeat village gossip: Mr. Mbuthia bought the junky car as a symbol for his son. He wanted the boy to brag in the future that his father had once owned a car.

No other family in the village, including mine, dreamed of cars. In my formative years, I never met a stranger in a car. Good rich people owned cars. They gave rides only if they pitied a peasant's tired limbs. Years later, while I lived in Nairobi, my life changed beyond my expectations. I owned a car and gave rides to many people.

On my flight to the United States, I interacted with strange people through several plane layovers. When I arrived at Lindbergh Field (Airport), San Diego, a strange man came to pick me that late evening. He could have done anything he wanted and claimed he never saw me.

When I accepted the rides, it had been two years since I arrived in the USA. The people I met had been strangers. The interesting thing: The ones, who had hurt me, through their words or negative impact on my life, were the ones I considered non-strangers. They had been in offices, school, malls, and at or around my residence. Even when I review my life pre-USA—in Solai, Nakuru, and in Nairobi—the people—strangers, family members, friends, and acquaintances—who tripped me and made my life harder, did not do so in the process of giving me a ride.

Chapter 14

Any Job Will Do

I did not get a single offer for a ride to the jobs the temporary agencies sent me. I left my apartment by 6:00 a.m., many times rode two buses to get to the job. At 4:00 p.m., I left work and headed to college for my evening classes, which ended at 10:00 p.m. The last bus dropped me at Fifth Avenue and Broadway after 11:00 p.m. I walked home along First Avenue. Occasionally, a police patrol car cruised behind me. When I turned and noticed the vehicle, I plodded along uninterested. In about a minute, the occupants would lose interest and drive away.

At my apartment, I ate food from my weekend cooking, watched a half-hour of TV, freshened and turned in for the night. On weekends, I studied, researched at the library, did household chores, and socialized with Ms. Psychologist's family.

Exhaustion did not bother me. My distress came from lack of steady work to pay my basic bills and stay in school. Between school, rent, food, transportation, plus miscellaneous expenses, my insurance settlement dried up. Temporary jobs had become slimmer as the Christmas holiday approached. It seemed I spent half of the business hours looking for work.

Those mini blackouts I experienced in Nairobi after my mother's death, returned with a vengeance. I consulted a doctor. He ran blood tests. After the results, he said nothing ailed me, and then added, "If there is anything wrong with you, I'm not the doctor to consult." He did not say what other type of doctor to consult.

In my mind that settled it. My problem dwelt in my head.

*

Head problem or not, I still needed to eat. My spirits rose when I called the agency one morning, but they subsided when the receptionist said she would send me for a week's phone operator job. "I'm not suitable for such a job. I've never worked on a switchboard," I said. But the main reason, although embarrassed to tell her, I knew callers and I wouldn't understand each other's accents. I preferred typing and filing—that sort of thing—not much speaking required.

"They will show you how to operate the switchboard. Remember to take your time card. Do you have one?"

"Yes." I took the job, afraid to jeopardize future assignments if I turned it down.

*

I walked the couple of blocks from my apartment to the publishing company, at the corner of Sixth Avenue and A Street. That turned out the best part of that job. I did not need to ride on those meandering San Diego buses. Although the bus ride was just half the problem, one had to have a car to earn the agencies' respect and get a posting.

It seemed skills amounted to little without a car. I missed several jobs until I learned how to lie on job applications. I recall one agency rep going through my application, nodding at intervals, and saying, "Your skills are perfect for this job." A paragraph down, she asked, "You don't have a car?" From then on, wherever the question, "Do you own a car?" appeared, "Yes" became my default answer. I ended with jobs all over town.

*

The woman who came to fetch me at the publishing company's reception said, "You're here already? I just called them. Come with me."

She escorted me to a tiny switchboard room, a floor or two up. When open, the door to the room almost touched the operator's chair. A woman we found answering calls sprang to her feet, removed the control from over her head and handed it to my trainer, and left.

In between fielding calls, the trainer pointed to the buttons that lit when calls came in. "All you do is press the lit button, answer, and forward the call to the recipient in this list." She handed me a list of employees with their extensions. "When extensions are busy, put incoming calls on hold using this button," she pointed. "And don't forget to forward the calls in the order they came in."

She pointed to a name on the phone list, "Call me on this extension if you've got a question."

"It's my first time to work on a switchboard," I said, hoping she would stay longer in case I made a mistake. At the same time I felt apprehensive that her watching over my shoulder would add to my anxiety.

"You will be okay."

"I hope so."

"Oh, sure." She handed me the phone control.

Before long, calls streamed in and overwhelmed the rookie. My brain and ears miscommunicated—the brain mixed-up or failed to discern what the ears heard. The callers asked for names I could not trace on the employees' list. Maybe she forgot to give me a second list. That had to be. Well, time to get creative. When I failed to guess a name, I forwarded the call to a random extension, hoping the receiver would forward it to the intended recipient. Within an hour, the job so rattled me I made a mental note to call in sick the following day.

Torture eased when two callers asked for familiar names back-to-back. No matter how nasal the callers got, they could not mangle names like West or Smith. Before I became comfortable, however, unbeknown to me, my undoing entered the building.

When the next call came, I did not quite get the name of the person the caller wanted. I put the caller on hold while I fumbled, my index finger going down the list to locate a name similar to what I thought I heard. When I reached the bottom of the list, without a possible match, I pressed on-hold button to clarify the name with the caller. The line had gone dead. Other calls came in, buttons flashed or beeped to indicate calls that had waited too long. I forgot the one that got away. After some minutes, a caller sounded agitated, stressed each word in a whispery tone. He said, "'Mr. Greensburg' isn't the type of person to keep waiting. He can't wait anymore." And the line went dead.

I did not quite understand the rushed complaint. Nonetheless, I panicked, without knowledge of what wrong I had done so I could right it. I later found out the receptionist was the one who had called, first to announce Mr. Greenberg's arrival to see the big boss and second, to complain about the delay.

The receptionist must have alerted someone else because just then the office went abuzz, similar to an attacked beehive. The news went from mouth to mouth about Mr. Greensburg—of all people— kept waiting by the new temp. Incredible! In the fracas, someone alerted the big boss upstairs, perhaps the only person who could appease Mr. Greensburg. Meantime, pecking hurried strides reached where I sat by the switchboard.

"What did you do? Do you know who you kept waiting?" Ms. Trainer asked, bending over the switchboard as if looking for clues.

I kept mum, clueless. I never got a chance to learn of the important fella I kept waiting.

The boss took charge. He could not trust any phone lines or anybody else. He trotted down the stairs to the reception area. On his way, his tirade filled the corridor. I heard his subordinates try to soothe him about the new temp employee. By the time he neared where I stood by the door, he stated he did not want to hear any explanations. "Whoever is on that switchboard better clear out. I don't want to ever hear about her in this company again."

The agency took me off its rolls.

*

Oh well, I had warned the agency of my inadequacy. Not to worry, temporary agencies are not like credit bureaus or insurance companies who go behind your back and share your shortcomings with others. My name remained in good standing at two other agencies. Before long, one of them sent me to California Newspapers Service Bureau (CNSB) for two-weeks, another no-transportation-needed job.

*

CNSB occupied a ground floor office in an old dingy building by the courthouse between Broadway and C Street. The office was a branch of a bigger company in Los Angeles, which advertised legal notices—trustee sales, probate, bulk sales, liquor licenses, and such. The branch office turned out to be a glorified, dimly lit typing sweatshop, with metal file cabinets aligning one wall. Everyone from the manager to a part-time college student occupied one large room, each seated at a dark wooden desk that would have needed four men to move. They worked on IBM golf-ball typewriters that caused such a racket a recruit needed to acclimate to concentrate. Many times the women skipped lunch to meet the never-ending advertising deadlines.

The work sucked me right in; not once did my mind stray when at work. Just the place I needed to prove my worth. The two weeks flew by. Kathy, the manager, said my work impressed her and if I had not come through an agency, she would have recommended to the head office in Los Angeles that they offer me a fulltime job.

"I can return to apply for the job later," I said.

"That'd violate the agency's contract with CNSB," Kathy said.

I wished she had kept her mouth shut. I felt all grateful for the two-weeks of work until she stoked my appetite for a fulltime job. Circumventing agency contracts did not feel upright, but it was hard for me to keep clean hands on an empty stomach.

*

The CNSB part-time pay helped me pay December rent. It gave me enough time to focus on where to get my January rent. But according to the agencies, employers had filled in their holiday positions and would resume hiring in the New Year. Newspaper ads yielded no jobs either.

Without job prospects, I sat back, contemplated and waited, calling an agency every other day. Two weeks went by. Mid-

December, my phone rang. I did not think much of it—I had given up on a job until the New Year. I answered.

"It's Kathy from CNSB."

My breathing stopped for a second.

"We were very impressed with your work. We'd like you to come work for us," she said.

"Oh!" I then capped the phone receiver to muffle my heavy breathing while I did several mental somersaults, my eyes closed.

"Are you still looking for a job?"

"Yes. What about the agency?" I asked after my voice calmed.

"I have already settled with them. When can you start?"

"Anytime." I hoped that did not sound too desperate.

Kathy got quiet for a minute. I heard papers rustle, "How about the nineteenth?"

I nodded. Oops! "Yes, that's fine."

"I will see you then."

On December 19, 1986, all suited in a blue skirt-suit bought from Goodwill Industries, I reported to my first fulltime job in America. The experience felt different, like admittance into an exclusive club—a member of the United States of America workforce.

*

Just days before Christmas, holiday festivities cheer—lights on building, residences, bridges, boats, and trees—dominated the city. I wanted to be in a festive mood and celebrate the holidays and my new job. With no wages yet, however, I had no money for a holiday feast let alone the forthcoming January rent. Maybe I could go to the Civic Center where the Salvation Army fed the homeless and family-less people during Christmas. No, I could not do that—that is for really poor or destitute people. Well, they feed the broke and the lonely, too. I could not bear the shame. I brushed that aside without a second thought. How about Ms. Psychologist's—she always welcomed me. No, I hated to seem needy.

Instead, I spent Christmas in my apartment watching TV and mulling over my life, thankful I had a job to look forward to in the New Year.

On December 27, lonely and with an anguished heart, I bought myself a belated Christmas gift—a Holy Bible, Old and New Testaments, the King James Version—a book I had never owned.

I read from Genesis, determined for once to read the book to the end, and hoping the insights would reveal a way to help me ease my then poverty-stricken state. Before I progressed too far into the book, I pledged to ignore any author who advised a reader not to worry about worldly riches: the, *it's easier for a camel to pass through the eye of a needle…* analogy. What was a world without its riches? I did not want to die before I enjoyed some of our world's good living.

The convoluted biblical tribal lineage fell on the wayside once I returned to my job at CNSB after Christmas.

*

Kathy trained me in trustee sales advertising, the only area I had not worked on during my two-week temp job. "I need you to be familiar with everything we do so you can pick up the slack," she said. A tall, bespectacled middle-aged white woman, the good kind, wore a short blonde hairstyle that trailed off at the back. Despite her above-average size, she always displayed a mild-manner, never raised her voice, or became visibly angry. She worked with gusto, which put pressure on me not to let her down.

Yolanda, the assistant manager, turned out feisty, quick-mouthed, a skinny Latina woman with a black boyish haircut. Her brain may have been quicker than Kathy's, but her heart a tad less generous. I got in a fight with her occasionally—I do not recall about what. She hurled words at me across the huge office we later moved into on the third floor of a four-story office building on Fifth Avenue and Beech Street. Shouting an argument twenty-five feet away proved exhausting. She once walked to the center of the room toward my direction, for better effect. Kathy did not intervene; she let our fights exhaust themselves.

Kathy was like that. She never blabbed about the goings on in the office. Sometimes I came in the morning and found an employee gone. That was how the probate woman I relieved for two weeks, while on vacation, left the company. I took over her probate and other miscellaneous tasks. I only helped with the trustee sales when Kathy and Yolanda got swamped.

John filled a vacancy left by another woman. He was young, maybe mid-twenties, skinny, as if not done growing. He was…I'm thinking…like the twin brother of Dr. Sheldon Cooper of the TV show *The Big Bang Theory*. I liked John. We discussed non-work matters that the others knew little about.

One day, I stayed late to finish probate forms I needed to file at the courthouse the following morning. John remained at his desk when the other employees left. He doodled on his blotter, making a comment now and then. I wrapped my work faster than before; our big boss in the head office in Los Angeles had retired our IBM typewriters and had computers installed.

John came and leaned on my desk. He told me, he and his older friend and others had made a round trip to London the previous weekend.

It sounded reckless. Why would he, a mere clerk, make such a trip while he had to work on Monday?

John talked about the plane ride, the party, the drinking, and the loaded friend. He made it sound wild and exciting.

"John, if I were you, I'd ask the rich friends to get me a better job so I can fit better in their company."

"But, he is my boyfriend," John said.

I gasped, but remained quiet, unsure of what to tell him.

John's eyes widened and his face turned crimson.

A pause.

"I'm gay," he said softly.

"I see." The usual "see" when I do not know what to say. What I saw did not matter back then, but my reaction choked our office friendship dead. Except the usual hello in the mornings, John and I never exchanged stories again. I saw him years later after his bones filled up. He looked a cultured grown man. We eyed each other from afar, without courage to approach and speak.

*

John was the only man who worked as a clerk. Another man conducted trustee sales all over the county, including the one in front of the courthouse at 220 Broadway. When auctions from different lenders overlapped, Kathy filled in for him at the courthouse. She took me to watch her conduct an auction a handful of times. One day, she said I needed to learn the last step of trustee sale—the auction. My nervousness started just before we left our office on Fifth Avenue. When I voiced it, Kathy assured me, "I'll be right there with you."

There I stood in front of the courthouse, overlooking Broadway. Investors waited in anticipation, their cashier's checks in hand, hoping to snap an underpriced property. A few people hung around to watch. Meantime, court employees, guests, and attorneys rushed in and out of the building.

After Kathy verified the bidders' checks, it was time for me to start announcing the first property's address, the minimum bid, and other terms and ask for bids. She stood beside me, like a watchful mother hen. The minute I started reading, a spike of warmth rushed through me. My voice quivered, my heart raced, and my legs threatened to give way until the last property. Although Kathy did not criticize my performance, we both realized I was not up to the task. That was my first and last auction.

*

At CNSB, I felt valued and respected. In thirty years, it remains the only place in the United States that I never felt a hint of bias, put-down, suspicion, or my abilities doubted. I strutted in the office or on my way to file papers at the courthouse while suited in professional attire. Kathy occasionally inquired, "Where do you buy your beautiful skirts and jackets?" Her more expensive drab-looking wear was no match to my inexpensive fitted look.

"You like this?" I would say, twisting my torso right and left, my eyes following along.

"Yes. And your other clothes, too. They fit you like tailor-made."

"Wow! You think so? Thanks."

I never disclosed my shopping alleys, embarrassed of people knowing I wore second-hand clothes. It was akin to poverty. I never let even my friend Lukia get wind of it. She looked down on used clothes and never imagined herself in thrift stores. Her mother sent her money from Uganda. Over the years, before I upgraded to new clothes, I gave her two of my Goodwill skirts she admired.

Used clothes or not, in 1987, I woke up every morning eager to go to work. In my weekly two to three courthouse visits, sometimes I sat in court with a copy of a document I had filed, just in case the court had misfiled the original. When this happened, the judge, leafing through the file, would tell the attorney, "This case shows no proof of advertising." When the attorney became disoriented, I flashed out a court-stamped copy before he blamed it on those inefficient advertising companies.

I interacted with array of people—paralegals, attorneys, newspaper personnel, heirs, and members of the public—mainly on the phone. CNSB sent me to paralegal lunch gatherings, hoping to get increased legal advertising from attorneys. That was a waste— going to gatherings made me uncomfortable, too shy to network. The best way we got our business was through word of mouth, at least in San Diego. Clients who did business with our office knew how meticulous we were in our work. Our office never put up with errors since no matter how slight, any mistake invalidated a document. This resulted in a new or multiple newspaper publications, delay, aggravation, and cost.

The only rub, my services went for cheap. I earned about $ 6.75 an hour. My take-home pay was just enough for shelter and basic living expenses. My income could not pay for my classes, or the balance of tuition I owed.

I dropped out of graduate school.

Chapter 15

Business and Education

During a stroll around University Town Center (UTC), I ran into Mr. Savior, whom I had not seen for some months. We interacted as acquaintances, without a hint of our former relationship and abusive past. The only thing he had done, however, was tell my friend Lukia that he would have liked to rekindle our relationship. But, despite his help after my mother's death, and the one-week I hibernated in his college apartment, I wanted nothing to do with him.

"Where have you been?" he asked. "I haven't seen you on campus lately."

"Oh…I dropped out," I said.

"You dropped out? What's the matter?"

"I got too busy."

He squinted. "Too busy to learn?"

"I'll return in a few months."

We indulged in more small talk before we exchanged phone numbers and parted.

Behind my back, Mr. Savior spread his charm to get me back to school.

Meantime, without school, I had enough spare time to devote to money search. I planned to start a small business—buying second-hand clothes from *Goodwill* and selling them at the swap meet, Saturdays and Sundays. If the business thrived, I would pay my bill at USIU and resume school in the fall.

I had married thrift stores by then.

*

The previous year, before I joined CNSB, Ms. Psychologist, my constant family and friend, must have noticed how I struggled to accomplish an office look. She suggested I go to a thrift store.

"What's a thrift store?" I asked.

"Where they sell used clothes. I will take you there Saturday if you like."

Back then, when we entered the *Goodwill* store, which was then located at the northwest corner of Fifth and Island Avenues, four blocks from my studio, it looked like a mini-mall. I recalled how I overpaid for beat-up clothes at a student's garage sale at USIU. Nice blouses (better quality than the two new ones I bought at Kmart for $12.50 apiece), cost only $2 to $2.50. Jackets and dresses went for $3.50.

I had splurged. For $10, I bought a navy-blue skirt-suit and two beige blouses for when I had to give an occasional college class presentation. I wore that suit the first day I reported to work at CNSB.

*

To launch my new business, I bought fifty neutral color, pastels, and striped blouses at $2.50 apiece, a few at a time. I also bought twenty new sweaters, one six-foot long aluminum clothes bar hanger, and a four-way collapsible one from the Los Angeles garment district. Between merchandise, hardware, supplies, and preparation, my budget of $150 had tripled by the time I set up shop.

Lack of a car could not dampen my enthusiasm. Ms. Psychologist dropped my wares and me at the Kobey's Swap Meet on Sports Arena Blvd. I doubt we discussed the duration of the drop-off, or pick up afterward.

My stall occupied a strategic space among new merchandise. My sociable neighbor sold new clothes. He schooled me on the ins and outs of swap meet business—the best spot, how to tell genuine customer from browsers by their body language, and so forth. I also took breaks under his tented stall where we traded stories between customers—his not mine.

By the time the swap meet closed at 3:00 p.m., I had sold only two blouses for $8. People looked, but walked away when they sported the hand-written homemade tags. The two blouses had cost me $5 and the rental space $15, resulting in a loss of $17, not counting my labor and transportation. My neighbor said it was a slow day. And although I didn't lose hope, I felt like a rejected suitor.

He offered to drop me home on his way to Chula Vista where he lived. He also said he would give me rides home as long as someone else dropped me in the mornings. I accepted the generous offer. Well, my first day of business did not end as badly as I feared at first.

The following week, I sold one blouse and none the next. As my swap meet neighbor drove me home, we brainstormed on how to improve my business. That day he helped me unload and carry my merchandise indoors. I offered him a seat and a glass of cold apple juice. While we discussed pros and cons of a swap-meet business, he said, "You can't manage a business on a bus."

"I know that." I did not need a self-styled swap meet businessman to rub it in. I had already concluded my venture was likely doomed.

"Maybe you need to think about it some more," he said.

Trust people to think you have not racked your brain raggedy already. "I'm doing the best I can. Do you have any suggestions?"

"Let's go into partnership, support each other," he said.

"How?"

"We combine our two businesses."

If we combined our businesses, he said, he would leave Chula Vista, ten miles away, at 6.30 a.m. and pick me at 7.00 a.m., Saturdays and Sundays.

"I will think about it," I said, uneasy of being tied to someone.

We exchanged phone numbers.

He called me on the phone twice the following week. He wanted friendship intertwined with business. I turned down the offer and phased out the business through garage sales, selling at cost, or cheaper in case of sweaters. I stopped all sales in another two months. Good thing the blouses fit me—I did not buy another blouse for the next six years. When I became tired of wearing any of them, I donated it back to Goodwill Industries. As I write this, decades later, there remains a white blouse and a beige sweater still hanging around among my clothes.

*

After winding down my business, I vowed to find a better way to increase my income. Like on cue, the phone rang one afternoon. When I answered, Mr. Savior bounced into my life again. He asked for my address. "I have a message for you," he said.

"Okay. What's the message?"

"I'd better come and tell you in person." That was how he had put it when my mother died.

"I hope nobody has died."

"Oh! No! No! I just think it's better that way."

Nothing that important came to mind, but I never underrated Mr. Savior. I gave him my studio apartment's address.

When he entered, he did not take the seat I offered. Instead, he put his left hand in his pocket while the right twirled his car keys as he walked around the small apartment like a house inspector.

The neat freak must have thrived on keeping women on the ready. Two years earlier when he and I used his apartment as our private dominion, he had no use for college sleep-ins. I can still recall our Saturday or Sunday ritual. We lay in bed, warm and snug at 6.30 a.m. He shed his side of the bedding and said, "It's time to get up." I grumbled when he got out of bed, letting a rush of cold air fill the vacuum. I then gathered the corners of the covers, clenched them closer to my chin as I settled in, making throaty coos.

An hour later, "Are you still asleep?" jarred me from my slumber. When I raised my head, my eyes assaulted by the light, I saw him adjust a corner of his eyeglasses. He sat at his desk, dressed in ironed jeans, spotless sneakers, and his signature long-sleeved shirt, sleeves folded halfway. An open textbook and a note pad on hand. He always studied for one to two hours before the weekend breakfast at 9:00 a.m.

At my Front Street apartment, my eyes followed his movements. *How dare he*!

After his assessment, he stopped twirling his keys and sat down. But not like regular humans. He perched his rear on the big couch's armrest.

"The last time we met, you informed me you had dropped out of college. That disturbed me," he said.

"I didn't mean to concern you with my troubles." Lay off my business, Mr. Patronizer, I felt like telling him, but instead I said, "I intend to resume classes in due course."

"I have been consulting with Dr. Phillips about that." Dr. Randall Philips was the Vice-President of Student Affairs at USIU. "And I have good news for you."

"It's about time I received good news." I let out a series of soft chuckles.

"Dr. Phillips got someone to pay two-thirds of your college tuition."

I gasped; my mouth remained closed, speechless. Two-thirds school assistance, just like in high school—(a story for another book)—became too much for me.

"The person wants to remain anonymous. He has already paid the two-thirds. In future, you only pay one-third."

My eyes pooled and my vocal cords refused to co-operate. I shook my head in disbelief. Talk of unexpected America. I overlooked to thank the miracle worker, bearer of sometimes sad and, other times, great news. He excused himself, and left.

With a lighter financial load, I returned to college in the fall of 1987, paid my tuition in dribbles and plodded along.

*

Two years after Mr. Savior completed his doctoral program, and before he returned to Kenya, I ran into him several times. Once I accompanied him to his company's party. He came to pick me in a sleek car I suspected he borrowed from his boss. The lady of the house I lived in at the time gave him one look and when I returned from the party, she said, "Wanjiru, you let such a man slip away!"

Whenever he and I saw each other, we never mentioned the past, or my scholarship. The last time I heard of him—after eighteen years—was when his former American friend asked about him. I checked the internet. A website listed him as an executive director of an international company in Kenya.

Chapter 16

Friends and Neighbors

For a working student, I lived in an ideal apartment, but some of my neighbors were not model citizens. What happened outside my doorstep concerned me after the manager told me about the getting-on and falling-off-the-wagon residents' backgrounds.

Take the gay couple in the apartment behind mine. The overweight "woman" partner was the only other black person I saw in the building. He did their household chores and ran errands. His partner, a soft-spoken average-size Hispanic man, went out to work. Mr. Woman claimed his partner was too passive, did not take initiative, and needed managing. As a caring "spouse," he had taken upon himself, he said, to file a job-related lawsuit on behalf of his partner. He mentioned other lawsuits he had filed in the past. It sounded as if most of the money management in the relationship fell on him.

One day, Mr. Woman knocked on my door. When I opened, he said, "I want to talk to you, if that's okay."

What did he want? We exchanged pleasantries when we ran into each other on the porch, but I did not want him to come to my apartment. I opened the door, "Come in." After he entered, I left the door open halfway, without offering him a seat.

"I notice you don't have a boyfriend. I'd like to help," he said.

I half-sighed in relief. At least he did not want to borrow money. I do not know what I project, but I have been a lender or donor since I became an adult. If I had five dollars in my pocket, a borrower who needed one or two dollars, or a trickster to claim the whole amount, would come along.

Maybe he is "bi," dips it forwards and backwards. Otherwise, why would he think he could help me in relationship matters?

"Help with what?"

"I'm not a jealous person. So, I don't mind sharing 'Jose' with you. I've already asked him. He doesn't mind."

"What made you think of that?"

"Well, what are neighbors for? I don't want you all lonely in here."

"I s-e-e," I said, confused about where to take the conversation.

"Okay, when you are ready, let me know, and I'll set you up."

"Thank you for stopping by. See you around."

After he left, I chuckled in amusement, and shook my head. It had to be one of those freaky things that happen in one's life. I remained iffy about his lifestyle—they were the first gay couple I met. Although by then it did not spook me like John's disclosure at CNSB.

*

Summer of 1987 was full of cheer. With a job and prospects of resuming my studies, my life under control. I had concluded my neighbors were okay people, "Trying to straighten their lives," the resident manager had said. I agreed with him because, despite their self-abuse history, except for an occasional beer bottle thrown in the side yard, none of them interfered with my peace and quiet.

That summer, I went on my first real American vacation. Through USIU's travel desk, seven students and I rented a van. Three experiences remain in my mind about that trip: We first stopped in Phoenix, Arizona, to savor the sights. When we got off the van, a wave of heat enveloped us as if we had entered a hot oven. The heat became so overwhelming we wanted out of the city. We rushed into a liquor store, bought cold drinks and hurried back to our air-conditioned van.

When we arrived at the Grand Canyon, we forgot all that heat. Overlooking the rusty awe-striking gorge arose a feeling in me similar to one I felt when I first looked down the Great Rift Valley— the wonders of nature and how miniscule we humans are in the larger scheme of things. Students took pictures from every angle. Two of them paid for a helicopter ride around the canyon.

We spent a night at a hotel, but all that is a blur. What I recall is our next stop, where students could not wait to get to—"Sin

City"—Las Vegas. As I understood it, on our drive home after our experience in the "Sin City," we should have gone to the Grand Canyon only. At the time, USIU had outlawed students' trips to Las Vegas, reportedly because a Japanese student had gambled and lost $30,000 in one weekend.

Squandering tuition and living expenses was not unusual. Some students did it through shopping, trips, or alcohol and drugs. It amazed me that parents could dispatch their young sons and daughters, fresh from high school to a foreign country, with money to act as surrogate family and support system.

Anyway, the Las Vegas buzz had rubbed on me that first trip. When we arrived that evening, I was more than ready to get initiated as a gambler. The other students, all Europeans, seemed as eager to get it out of their system before they returned to their home countries.

At the casino entrance, our group agreed to disperse and reassemble the following morning. Without prior slot machine knowhow, I first familiarized myself by sitting or standing by low-level gamblers. They never seemed to mind me because of how they focused on pulling levers of those juke-box-size slot machines. I felt like a spectator at the middle of a gigantic disco, with lights and dancing machines going *ching-ching!* When I felt confident enough to start on my quest to riches, I had the good sense to treat myself first to an inexpensive buffet dinner.

With a satisfied stomach and somewhat settled in, I changed $20 into quarters—80 quarters seemed right to get me going. At one time, a stream of shiny silver coins clicked and clanked into the receptacle, filling it to the brim, with a handful of rogue ones escaping to the floor. Oh, the thrill of winning! More enjoyable and easier money than that silly swap meet business. It seemed with $20 I could win enough to cover the cost of my trip. After I determined a machine could spit money only so much, I changed to another one— my winnings heavy in a plastic bucket provided by the casino.

That move brought me bad luck. No sweat. I scouted and soon scooted over to a third machine, which seemed, perhaps because it looked prettier than the others did, as if it could bring me luck. It teased me, spit a few quarters here and there, but it failed to break my losing streak. By midnight, despite making two more changes, the machines had swallowed my precious quarters, even the extra loose ones I dug from my bag. The loss tempted me, but failed to coax me to dip into my pocket for another twenty. As someone said on TV, *when you have been at the bottom, you never forget it.*

The only snag was that our Las Vegas part of the trip did not include hotel accommodation. Through stories of glamor and potential riches, who needed sleep? (It never occurred to me, even for a minute, to wonder about a night of gambling.) So, I made do and took to the bathroom. One look and it seemed like what I had heard crowded jails look like after bars close on Saturdays. The awake, not too drunk, but tired or distraught, shared their evening's exploits—the fortunes won and lost. I listened and spent the rest of the night in the bathroom lounge, standing, squatting, or leaning against the wall.

I sat on a couch's armrest when another broke gambler freed it. The ones lucky to secure the couches leaned their heads back and slept. I saw none of them move unless a friend or relative stood by to trade places with.

I kept good company all right: old women haggling with their group whether they had enough dollars left between them to afford a room, or skimpily dressed young women, broke and drunk from the casino's free drinks. I never gambled enough to earn a free glass of wine from the young women servers who strolled around, identifying gamblers who qualified for the wine when their machines swallowed enough cash. Miserable, miserable anticlimax.

When my group reassembled in the morning, all looked haggard and grumpy from sleeplessness or loss of money. None of them shared a single story. I suppose they had to keep the Las Vegas mantra—what happens in Vegas remains in Vegas. Except that one half-night blemish, I enjoyed the trip a great deal.

*

That summer did not bring only smiles; some frowns came along, too. When people came out of their winter and spring cocoons, some travelled, others visited beaches and others barbequed and partied. My neighbors did their part. Some Saturday evenings, two young men sat on the front porch, a few feet from my front glass door.

Sometimes they invited friends, drank, smoked and, most likely, took drugs. It did not bother me. The small group cleared the porch by 9:00 p.m., perhaps for better excitement elsewhere. With extended daytime summer hours, however, they extended their drinking hours. For two Saturday nights, the young men had already ruled the porch area and adjacent parking lot. The manager did not interfere, or he could not hear the raucous from his back apartment.

Unlike the previous two times, when the noise stopped before I went to bed, one night, commotion of male voices awoke me at 1:00 a.m. The arguments escalated to stomps, grabs, and shoves. One man's footsteps paced up and down the sidewalk, and off the porch alongside my apartment. He issued threats of a beating he would give the other. The huge windows that flooded my studio with natural light during the day made me feel exposed. At one time, the commotion came so close to my main glass door I worried the men might break through.

When they moved farther down the porch, under cover of darkness, I tiptoed to the door, cracked the drape and peered. One man grabbed and pulled the sleeve and arm of another—both seemed young and underfed. Another man, out of view, continued with his drunken threats. I did not dare turn on the lights to check the manager's phone number in case I drew the men's attention. Calling the police did not cross my mind; I had never had to call them. With nothing else to do, I tiptoed back to my bed and kept vigil.

Sleep wrestled with me. It ended up winning, coming in fits the rest of the night, along with a dream. In the dream, the men broke my glass door and continued to punch, shove, and wrestle with each other around my bed as if I did not exist.

When I awoke at 6:00 a.m., all was quiet. I ventured out my door at 6.30. Except three empty beer bottles strewn on the grassy trail off the sidewalk, no other trace of the night's ruckus remained. The manager may have warned my two young neighbors because no such lively party took place for the rest of my stay in the building.

*

With calmer neighbors, job, and school, my life seemed normal, despite limited relationships. My classmate Dennis came to study with me some Saturdays. Although I spoke better English than he, I never quite understood why he believed he could study better with me than with a native English speaker. He came from Guadalajara, Mexico, born of a French father and a Mexican mother. Perhaps because he was tall and lacked a visible strand of Mexican trait, or because his looks commanded better treatment if he left out the Mexican part, he highlighted the French side of his family, although I doubt he spoke fluent French.

I did not realize, as innocent as our relationship was, that, besides Dennis giving me occasional rides to school, he acted as my gatekeeper until my neighbor, Mr. Woman, brought it to my attention when I ran into him at the front porch.

"I see you've a boyfriend now. I'm happy for you," he said. I smiled without acknowledging or denying his assertion. After that, he never mentioned sharing his Jose with me. And in time, we lost touch when I moved, and he embarked on other endeavors.

A decade later, while flipping TV channels, a familiar face caught my eye. I paused. An overfed man stood behind a podium, a huge sign of the cross on the wall behind him. His big frame overflowed with elaborate long robes—in whites, gold, and maroon. He faced his audience as kings did in Roman times. As the former Mr. Woman spoke, the worshippers before him raised their eyes to his imposing figure, as they eagerly awaited him to enlighten them and share his wisdom on the magnificence of the afterlife.

*

Despite Dennis helping keep nosy Mr. Woman—before his makeover—at bay, he, Dennis, could not shield me from everyone. In fall, just two months after the porch party, I returned from work and found my apartment looking like a tornado aftermath. Flabbergasted, I did not know what to make of it. The main door and the windows remained intact. In case someone still lurked inside, I walked around stealthily, the strap of my bag still slung over my shoulder in case I had to sprint outside. Clothes littered the floor— loose, on hangers, or in messy piles. Chairs and side tables lay upside down; half the windows had curtains pulled down; pots and pans heaped on the kitchen counter, drawers ajar. The kitchen table held four plates of spaghetti—two untouched and two half-eaten—with cutlery, and smears of ketchup, jam and butter. The out-of-sight bed remained the only item spared from the rampage. Yet, on scrutiny, nothing was missing except a necklace.

Unlike the party incident, this time I called the police. Meantime, the new resident manager appeared on the porch. "Someone vandalized my apartment. I've called the police," I told him.

"When?"

"While I was at work. Did you see anyone around here?"

"No, except your son. I let him in."

"What son? I don't have a son. I live alone."

"How should I know?"

"Then, why did you open for him?"

"Well, a teenage boy introduced himself as your son and told me he forgot his key when he left for school this morning. I wasn't going to let the poor boy wait until you came home."

To the manager's credit, he said he asked the boy some question, and he knew all the pertinent information about me. From the manager's description, I recognized the culprit. Two years earlier, when I babysat him and his brother, he had packed his small suitcase with a $20 bill in hand to go buy an air ticket to accompany me to my mother's funeral in Kenya. The boy liked me; I failed to understand—although I suspected psychological issues—how he could vandalize my apartment.

I felt violated, and confused on how best to handle the matter. "I'll hold management responsible for the damage," I told the manager.

I thought of cancelling the call to the police after I learned what had happened, but feared the police might accuse me of filing a false claim and wasting police precious time. I would also need evidence if I were to ask management for clean-up compensation.

Before long, two police officers arrived. I told them what the manager said. One of them surveyed the damage while the other interrogated me. In less than five minutes, I regretted my rush to call them before I reported the incident to the manager. That was my second experience with the San Diego police. It reminded me of two patrol officers' conduct when I worked as a babysitter for Ms. Psychologist.

My two charges—my now apartment wrecker and his younger brother—and I sat by the fountain facing Broadway in front of Horton Plaza, before the owners remodeled it to its current look. While the boys ate hamburgers they had barraged me to buy, two police officers strolled around leisurely, one about six feet behind the other. The front one tapped his baton on his left palm in slow motion. He smirked, cocked his head toward us and said, "This must be their only meal for the day."

I missed his partner's reply. They chuckled and continued their little entertainment farther from us.

If I have a problem, I would hate to have those police officers come help me, I thought back then. But they were not the ones who came two years later after the vandalism. The department sent one black officer and one white. The white one inspected the damage while his partner interrogated me. He invaded my space, towered over me, his arms akimbo. He rained questions on me, framed them three different ways, as if I had vandalized my own residence. It agitated me, and I felt taken for a fool.

The officers finished in about half an hour. They did not haul me to the police station, which I had feared. I went there in three days—to collect a police report.

When my neighbors learned the resident manager had opened the door for the wrecker, they drooled at the get-rich-quick opportunity at my disposal. The previous manager told me, "Sue them. You may very well end up owning this building."

Fortunately, for the building owner, my parents never trained me to leech on others, believing you earned your keep through sweat from your own brow. But with scary weekend parties and vandalism, the ideal, affordable apartment had turned ugly. I felt also that my neighbors' lifestyles fell short of what I aspired to. The dilemma: stay put, or move to a better residence and not afford my one-third college tuition. I searched my soul: why could I not be content as I saw many people live and do their best with what they had? With my clerical duties and a well-located studio, I just needed to keep to myself, I reasoned. The people in the building would not harm me.

If they did, it would not be intentional. But soul search or not, the part of me I can't tame or explain, refused to settle, kept on craving for more. I started searching for another residence.

Chapter 17

It's Nana Not Grandmother

My friendship with Ms. Psychologist flourished despite her son's assault on my apartment. She searched alongside me for a room-for-rent. Her friend, Mrs. Greer, needed someone to rent a room in her three-bedroom, two-story house in Skyline Hills. Ms. Psychologist set a meeting for Mrs. Greer and me. To my surprise and relief, Mrs. Greer agreed to rent to me even before we met. As her grandson put it months later, "She was happy to help a sister from the continent."

When she and I met, her terms sounded too generous. I worried she might increase the rent after I moved in. Nonetheless, I gave my 30-day notice to move out of my studio apartment.

*

Mrs. Greer did not change her mind or the terms of the room rental. She assigned me to wash pots and pans and load the dishwasher after dinner. The few chores plus the downstairs furnished bedroom and board cost me $32.50 per week. She turned down my request to pay rent bimonthly, to correspond with my pay periods, saying, "Weekends are when I shop for groceries." Months later, she told me she received a Federal Government pension and Social Security payment at the beginning of the month. By the fifteenth, she ran out of money. My pittance rent paid for groceries the rest of the month.

The widow occupied the master bedroom upstairs, and her two great-grandsons, seven and eight, had the bedroom opposite. Mrs. Greer—or "Nana," as she soon told me—came downstairs to get her mug of coffee, then watched TV shows in her bedroom all morning, occasionally smoking skinny brown cigarettes before she quit. Afternoons, she ran errands or played dominos seated at the dining table with friends, or Nintendo, before she cooked dinner. Sundays were her church days where she volunteered four hours during the week.

The boys called her Nana. I did not think it appropriate to address her that way. So, I addressed her as Mrs. Greer, which became stifling within two weeks. Not long after, I called one boy and told him, "Go tell your grandmother...." I omitted "great"—it sounded too old. When Mrs. Greer came downstairs, she said to call her Nana, not grandmother. Three generations of young mothers had catapulted her to great-grandmother status, a role she sounded neither ready for nor willing to acknowledge in her mid-sixties. Unbeknownst to her—and I did not dare tell—Nana means great-grandmother in Gikuyu, my native language.

Skyline Hills felt like home. Since I arrived in the United States, except Mr. Savior, Ms. Psychologist, Ms. Nutcase, and Dr. Therapist, I had not socialized or interacted with any other black people. The only awareness I had of the "black" community, came through TV police confrontations or movie actors and singers— groups far removed from my reality.

Unlike in Logan Heights with its small and medium-size aged houses, in Skyline, three to four-bedroom, two-story homes dominated the neighborhood, with a scatter of single-storied ones. People watered their lawns, others walked around the neighborhood and adjacent park in the mornings, and children walked to and from school. With strategic trees planted along the streets and backyards, the air smelled fresher, too. If I had to pick one time, I suspect my move to Skyline Hills, and in Nana's house in particular, was the point that America started to sprinkle its mystic on me. I then entertained the idea I could live in the USA for a few years before I returned to Kenya with pockets overflowing with dollars.

*

By 1988, I had assimilated into Nana's household. I ate healthier, too. She baked or broiled most of her foods except red snapper or catfish, which she deep-fried, and which I savored with relish without concern of its artery-clogging properties. Nobody baked chicken as well as she did, not even in restaurants I had patronized. I baked it when I moved from her house but never came close. Her cooking was not only pleasing to the eye and delicious to the mouth, but also appealing to the nose. Welcoming aromas filled her house and wafted to the yard when she made crunchy cookies sprinkled with nuts. And those pies! I sometimes took a slow deep breath, cooed with my eyes shut. Nana smiled, pride in her eyes, whenever I did this.

I recall no dinner of hers without dessert: ice cream, homemade apple or sweet-potato pies, savory chocolate-chip/nuts cookies, and cakes. She bought fruits sporadically. The boys ate them one-by-one when they played outside until they finished every one of them.

*

Despite our tranquil living conditions, Nana and I disagreed on two issues. She retired at sixty-two because, "I got tired of freeway driving," she told me. She preferred I keep her company some evenings. When I arrived home from work and school, I felt too tired for social interactions. I ate dinner, cleared the kitchen and loaded the dishwasher, ready to unwind in my bedroom while I watched my black-and-white TV. We socialized on limited basis or on weekends when I watched her big color TV by the fireplace we hardly lit, in the living room.

While my seeming aloofness bothered Nana, her behavior toward the boys disturbed me. Perhaps these problems existed even when I moved in, but, busy with my affairs, I did not pay attention. Or, as the boys grew older, they needed more discipline.

She clothed and fed the boys well, but criticized and blamed them for the simplest transgressions. If one of them took a soda from the refrigerator reserved for Nana's evening brandy cocktail (later, she hid her soda bottle under the kitchen sink where the boys never suspected), romped around and knocked something down, or talked back, a guaranteed tirade rained on him. It made me cringe to hear her put-downs, which sometimes included the boys' unplanned births, and what an imposition they were on her life. Every few months, when she got tired of the ineffective verbal abuse, she solicited the help of her grandson, the boys' maternal uncle. She never called for discipline assistance from their "stifling-know-nothing-bum" father, as she referred to him. They loved him, even if he did nothing for them. Functionally illiterate, he could not get or keep a job no matter how many times the government pushed him around for child support.

The boys were full of trembles when their special date with the uncle came. I had not figured why at first, when they acted unusually quiet during dinner. In my bedroom, with the TV on, I never heard the uncle when he jostled the two boys upstairs to their bedroom—always after dinner. He locked the door and whipped them with a leather belt. The first time I walked to the kitchen and heard commotion, I thought they were wrestling in their bedroom. But I heard thumps, muffled hollers, and whimpers—nothing loud enough for a neighbor to hear. I peered in the living room where Nana watched TV and asked her, "What's going on with the boys? Are they okay?"

"Yes, they are with their uncle," she said. "Since they didn't listen, they got what they had coming."

The other time I heard the beating; I hurried up the stairs, banged on the door, and told Mr. Grandson to "Stop it." The door remained locked, and my attempts went unheeded, but the beating trailed off soon after. When I brought it up during peacetime, Grandson and Nana defended their actions. At one time, Nana quoted that dimwitted Bible verse: *Spare the rod and spoil the child.*

I knew nothing then about Child Protective Services, but from what I heard when Nana goaded the boys, "Here is the phone. Call them and go to the System," I believed the boys were better off with her.

The fear of a child going to the "System" stayed with me until years later when I got into financial trouble for trying to help get a child out of it. In Nana's case, I looked the other way.

Chapter 18

Transportation

With three accomplishments—back in school, steady job, and an affordable stable home—I planned to buy a car. I had shed a tear or two when I missed a bus, waited an hour for the next one, and arrived late for my class.

I shared my car aspirations with my CNSB co-workers—Kathy and Yolanda. Kathy acknowledged my need without another comment, always the diplomat.

"You can't get a car loan without credit," Yolanda said.

Granted, I did not appreciate how critical good credit was. But accomplishing a goal I had set for myself, no matter how improbable it seemed to others, was part of my makeup. I believed there had to be a way to convince the car dealers I was worth their trust. My almost-one-year steady job and school attendance had to count for something.

Credit was not my only hurdle, but I kept that to myself, deciding to tackle each challenge when I got to it.

Ms. Psychologist, a doer by nature, agreed nothing was insurmountable. She drove me along the Mile of Cars, a whole mile lined with car dealerships on both sides, in National City. We visited several dealers, but failed to find a suitable economy car I could afford. We agreed to go home and try the following weekend. On our way home, just before we passed the last dealership, I said, "Slow down, slow down. That's the type of car I want," I pointed.

"Which one?" Ms. Psychologist said as she slowed down and looked. She pulled into a Ford Motors' dealership. By the time we exited the car, a tall brunette salesman stood by.

"Welcome, ladies," he said.

"How much is that car?" I asked, pointing.

"The Ford Festiva?"

"The small blue one."

"First drive it and see how it feels," he said. The three of us walked to the car.

I drove about four blocks. I loved the car's maneuverability, especially because I had not driven in three years, except once on USIU campus. Mr. Savior and I freaked out when I drove on the left, Kenya style, and did not realize it until a car faced us head on.

Back at the dealership office, seated at the salesman's desk, Ms. Psychologist helped me haggle on the price based on the $150 monthly payment I had budgeted. Before long, I realized the salesman's figures meant little; he presented any figure we came close to agreeing on to an out-of-sight manager. The salesman did this several times. What a tiresome practice! I would have walked away if I were not desperate for a car. It reminded me of bargaining in Nairobi, or Tijuana across the border in Mexico. In every case, I wondered whether I settled too soon when I felt tired and accepted the price. I vowed to avoid the practice when I became able to afford a better way of buying a car.

Finally, "Mr. Salesman" returned, grinning. Mr. Out-of-sight manager had approved a payment of $159 per month, nine dollars more than my budget. All I had to pay were taxes, insurance, and registration to take the car home. That suited me fine. Ms. Psychologist went to wait in her car while Mr. Salesman and I did the paperwork.

He asked for my W-2 tax form (a form that shows an employee's annual income) and my college transcript—proof I had a job and attended college, my claim for credit worthiness.

"I can get the transcript, but I don't have a W-2. I've been on my job for only ten months."

"I will have to ask my manager whether he can make an exception," Mr. Salesman said and disappeared again through the now familiar door.

I waited.

"I've good news," he said before he finished taking his seat. "You can bring three months' pay-stubs, college transcript, and your current driver's license."

"I can get a transcript and pay-stubs, but I have something to tell you."

"Shoot. I'm here to help."

"I don't have a California driver's license. Is that going to be a problem?"

"Ooooh! That's a big problem!" He leaned back in his chair and interlaced his fingers behind his head. "You can't finance a car or get auto insurance without a valid driver's license…. Do you know how to drive?" He rose to his feet.

"Yes, I know how to drive." Mr. Salesman did not seem to hear me, but I added, "I have a Kenyan driver's license." I doubted after three years in the USA the authorities would honor a foreign driver's license. I had planned to buy a car and then use it for my driving test.

Mr. Salesman nodded. I sensed it was not in acknowledgement to what I had just told him; he was in his private world. It seemed pointless to mention I had a California learner's permit. I expected him to terminate the sale and tell me to return after I got a California driver's license.

He did not.

"Your foreign driver's license is no good, but I'll think of something." He strolled around the showroom and out the exterior door, hands in his pockets.

I stayed put at his desk.

After he walked around for fresh air and thinking, he returned. "I'll tell you what; I will take you to DMV."

What a special offer! He really wanted to sell me that car. It had not escaped me that in over an hour, no other customer had appeared. That did not diminish the thanks I bestowed on him for his kindness.

*

On the day of the driving test, Mr. Salesman picked me by our office building on 5th Avenue and Beech Street. He drove north through Bankers Hill to the Department of Motor Vehicles (DMV) office on Normal Street in Hillcrest. The big parking lot was full. He pulled into the carport attached to the building where driving tests started. The inside of the building was abuzz. Current and future drivers lined, waiting for the counter clerks to call numbers—before efficient impersonal monitors took over. Others sat at desks taking written tests in the periphery. DMV was the one place in America, at least in California, except the immigration office, where one needed to carry lunch or a snack, unless one had an appointment. At night, the building looked like an abandoned old clubhouse, a haunted structure in the middle of an empty concrete lot.

Before the examiner came, Mr. Salesman showed me how to work his car controls. It helped little. The examiner noticed my nervousness when I entered and exited a highway. I missed two turning lanes and crossed solid lines to exit. Kenyan streets had no designated turning lanes. My mind raced—even before the examiner announced I had failed—I should have saved money and taken at least two driving lessons. I worried I had blown my chance to buy that small blue car.

I did not need to worry.

Mr. Salesman professed he would stand by "his woman."

I booked another driving test before he dropped me at my office.

He and I went an hour earlier for the second test. I practiced driving around the neighborhood hills and dips, Park Boulevard, University Avenue, and Highway 163. By the test time, I drove so well the examiner got carried away. "You're from Africa," he said. He went on to inquire about African culture and minerals—copper, gold, and diamonds. I indulged him in some African generalities—copper in Zaire, or was it Congo by now?—diamonds in South Africa, and so forth. I needed to read more on Africa because I was clueless or rusty on the things he wanted to know.

I passed the test, perhaps with an "A" or whatever highest mark DMV awards. I felt buoyed, wore a grin when Mr. Salesman and I talked like old buddies on our way back to his dealership to process my loan and insurance applications. After we signed the papers, he congratulated me and handed me the keys to the blue Ford Festiva, two-door stick-shift car. The man had gone beyond any buyer's expectations to make sure I bought that car.

When he walked me to the car, and just before I got in, he said, "It's really a *new* car."

"Of course it's a new car. What do you mean?" I asked.

"Somebody had it for a week but didn't hold his end of the bargain."

Then I recalled the first day Mr. Salesman took me for a test drive. I had asked him why the car's speedometer showed hundreds of miles.

"These miles add up," he had said.

Back then, I understood it to mean mileage accumulated from buyers' test drives, which, in my excitement, I did not stop to think and wonder.

Standing next to my *new* purchase, I paused for seconds. No wonder he worked double time to get me to purchase the car. Refusing to take the car did not cross my mind. I had cleared hurdles to buy it and might not have qualified for another.

"You are supposed to disclose before I buy."

"We had to get a lot done first, remember?"

What could I say to that? Nothing. Besides, I wanted to get out of there. Darkness had set in. And as if that were not enough, it started to drizzle. Mr. Salesman gave me directions. I hesitated. I could not picture Skyline Hills in my mind, and the neighborhoods in between were unknown to me. *Maybe call Ms. Psychologist to come take me home, and I pick the car the following day.* It had been only two months since I moved in with Nana; it did not feel right to impose on her. Besides, the exhilaration of owning my first car in the United States could not let me leave it at the dealership. I drove.

It is hard to see side streets' names at night, but driving through unknown streets in a drizzle became tricky. I feared I might wreck my car. I rolled my first car the third day after purchase in Kenya. That thirteen-year old experience resurfaced and grated on my mind. I pulled onto the side of a well-lit street and checked my watch. Twenty minutes gone, and I had no idea of my location.

One place I knew the general direction of was Ms. Psychologist's house in Logan Heights. Besides visiting her family on weekends, we drove from her house the first time she and I went to the Mile of Cars. If I drove northwards, I was bound to come to a familiar street that could lead me to her house. From her house, I could recognize the route to Skyline Hills.

In fifteen minutes, I came face-to-face with her house, and in another ten, I arrived home in Skyline Hills. Whew! I did not disclose my car tribulations to either Ms. Psychologist or Nana.

*

Owning a car was a necessity in San Diego, unlike in places with well-developed mass transits such as San Francisco or New York. Ten years later, before my niece Nancy bought a car, she told her father, "Living in San Diego without a car is like a person walking barefoot on the streets of Nairobi."

It felt great when I stopped being one of the "barefoot" people. The car helped me shorten my travel time, which previously took about a fourth of my day. It also let me get involved in activities outside my work and school. I rejoined the People-to-People

organization of which Dr. Randall Phillips was president. The
international organization connected diverse groups of people and
promoted peace. He visited Japan's Chapter often and, as president,
scouted quality speakers for the San Diego Chapter's monthly
meetings. Members met at one of the country-like buildings at the
USIU campus. Occasionally, the group met in Rancho Bernardo, to
give relief to North County members who drove longer distances
than the others did. Other times, rich members invited us to their
spacious homes, which turned out quite a treat for some of us.

Shortage of finances prevented me from attending other
meetings held outside San Diego, except once when Mariana and I
joined members and flew to a gathering in Hayward, Northern
California. The following day, Mariana turned sixteen. Dr. Phillips
gave her sixteen one-dollar bills. It became quite a conversation piece
when we learned of the practice of giving children gifts matching
their ages.

*

In all the years I knew Dr. Phillips, I showed him deference, but never
garnered enough courage to mention and thank him for the
anonymous scholarship he gave or solicited for me, without which I
would have cut my education short or delayed it. I honored him to
the end when I read about his death in U-T San Diego newspaper.
His family had not given the burial details, but they, together with
friends, had organized a memorial service at the Japanese Garden in
Balboa Park, adjacent to downtown San Diego.

When I arrived, at least 300 mourners congregated, wearing all black like in a daytime formal award ceremony. A handful of men wore yarmulkes. Most people stood listening to the service, overlooking the well-kept gardens next to the cafe near the Organ Pavilion, where visitors sit or hang around listening to free summer concerts or enjoying a cup of coffee in the tranquil surroundings. As a black person, and because I do not wear black clothes to funerals, I stuck out like a Playboy magazine pinned on a church bulletin board. With no one to share my sorrow, I stood at a distance. I heard murmurs only of people paying their tributes. It reminded me of the *Out of Africa* movie, featuring Robert Redford and Meryl Streep, in which a Somali woman watched from afar when a small group of people buried her boyfriend, "Bror."

I thanked Dr. Phillips, as I had done countless times, for contributing to my life and the lives of others. I left before the crowd dispersed and noticed my disconsolate presence.

Chapter 19

Foreclosure Condo

Besides going to activities I could not attend before, and cutting on my travel time, the car enabled me to visit friends like Esther. I had met her in Kearny Mesa at a company where we did clerical work during my temp-job days. She trained and became a real estate agent at about the same time CNSB gave me a fulltime job. While on a visit at her house in National City, she said with my steady job I could buy a property. The information whetted my curiosity. I had not expected to buy a property before I returned to Kenya, but if I bought one, maybe it would enable me to have a sizeable lump sum when the time came to leave.

Before Esther took me to view properties, she explained the purchase process. After offer and acceptance, she talked about escrow, termite and physical inspections, appraisal, title insurance, and a myriad of other requirements. It sounded mighty confusing. But Esther assured me she would explain the process as we progressed.

In the 1980s, buying a property in Kenya was simpler. After purchasers met the income and job requirements and paid their down payments, the developer handed the transactions to a lawyer to process and settle. When buyers signed title deeds and accompanying paperwork at the lawyer's office, the developer's representative took each buyer for a final walk-through and keys hand-over. Besides, it was uncommon for Kenyans to buy used houses, although this has changed. People in rural areas built and still build their own houses.

In San Diego, Esther first showed me a clean upstairs two-bedroom condominium (Condo) on Delta Street, by the border of San Diego and National City. The bank had repossessed the condo when the previous owner failed to make payments. Before she wrote the offer, a mortgage broker from her office qualified me for a loan. He asked about my income, paystubs, and checked my credit. When he confirmed I qualified for the condo, Esther wrote an offer on my behalf for the minimum bid of $40,000. My bid won. I paid $500, termed earnest money deposit.

During the loan process, I paid for a credit report and appraisal fees. I failed to understand why the bank required an appraisal while they owned the property, and they and I had agreed on the price. My credit report came out satisfactory because of the timely payments I had made for the car I bought the previous year. In three weeks, the mortgage broker submitted my loan to a lender for final approval.

When the lender's response came, I became even more confused. They approved my loan, but not the condo. They gave me six months to look for an alternative property. Why? I understood it later when I learned the class system and capitalism are intertwined.

Esther tried to convince me that my approval remained intact, that the condo was the problem—it didn't meet the bank's requirements. Her sales pitch did not console me. In my mind, I had already bought the condo, occupied the master bedroom, and sublet the second bedroom. The rent I planned to collect would have covered the mortgage with me paying the $150 homeowner association fees only. I found it hard to embrace another condo, felt like a member of a couple in love when a third person asserts, "You two aren't fit for each other."

What about the money I paid? I got back the $500 deposit, but credit and appraisal fees went bye-bye. The little soft voice inside me nagged me to abandon the purchase, and wait until I became conversant with real estate in America. I overruled the nag and stuck with Esther.

She took me to view another lender-repossessed condo in the same vicinity. It came "as is" with dents on walls and doors, and two broken windows. My inner voice gave me another kick: Do you remember Front Street? A flashback of those two young men flexing their limbs outside my former studio apartment went through my mind. That type of behavior would produce the damage on the walls of the condo we were viewing.

No matter how much Esther downplayed the cause of the damage, which she attributed to romping children, I refused to view more properties. When she insisted on taking me to a different neighborhood, I said I wanted to wait until I learned San Diego communities well and how properties changed ownership in California. Before we parted, I asked her the best way for me to learn real estate terms. She recommended a book on how to purchase a house.

After I read the library book, the house-purchase process remained fuzzy.

While with Esther and three of her colleagues, I asked where they trained as real estate agents. Esther gave me a convoluted story about job and real estate conflict. One of the other two women mentioned Anthony Schools. With a little research, I found a listing of the school in Chula Vista and in Clairemont. I went to the Chula Vista campus.

Real estate classes merged with my college studies, with a plan to complete both programs the same year. Anthony Schools required me to complete twelve subjects to take the California Real Estate Principles test, which included accounting, business practices, business law, zoning, and others. I took about a year to complete the course and take the state exam. I had already covered some of the material in college, but the school had a curriculum that one had to follow.

By the time I passed the California real estate license exam, I was familiar with the term *redlining*, neighborhood discrimination, the fate that befell the condo I first planned to buy. *Redlining* was against the law, but some lenders and real estate professionals still practiced it.

After I completed my college program and became a licensed real estate agent, I decided to practice real estate part-time to supplement my great-job but pathetic income at CNSB. Meantime, I continued to scout for a job geared toward a career elsewhere.

*

When I joined Esther at the office where she worked in National City, I soon learned a state license covered about five percent of what an agent or broker needed to know in real estate. The rest turned out to be on-the-job training coupled with workshops and seminars. The basics were how to write agreements, how to present them to sellers or buyers, how to overcome objections from prospects who needed to sign paperwork they didn't half-understand—especially first-time buyers and sellers—not to mention the changing legal requirements an agent had to keep up with. And the king or queen of them all, that determines whether a business lives or dies—how to get customers and clients.

I needed to learn as much of the ninety-five percent of the business immediately if I planned to make money in real estate. Although, from the office setup and only coming to the office evenings and weekends, I expected it would take me time to learn.

The broker of record should have taken me through an orientation. Instead, he told me to shadow other agents when they went to appointments or property showings. I floated around the office most evenings and weekends. No one wanted to adopt a shadow. My friend Esther ran around busy all the time and said she could not spare time to coach me.

From the beginning, I had noticed the clannish set-up in the office. Except the drop-in vendors, I remained the only non-Filipino. Many times, they spoke English as an afterthought. That did not concern me, at first. But in time, I felt sidelined. And with all the real estate theory in my head, and no skills of how to convert it to sales, I started looking for a more diversified office.

*

I attended an evening Career Day offered by the then largest office in National City. When I arrived there after work, the second floor office looked professional, with a large meeting room, windows facing National City Blvd. The eager fifteen-people group of hopefuls looked diversified.

The charismatic Mr. Q, one of the two owners, first introduced the company's accountant, a black man and a real estate broker. Mr. Q then summarized his presentation. He called listing properties the lifeblood of real estate. He talked about prospecting on a consistent basis, about sphere of influence, mass mailings, advertising in newspapers and magazines, involvement in social activities, door knocking, and cold calling.

Some terms were unfamiliar to us. Mr. Q explained that cold-calling meant contacting people one didn't know, and sphere of influence involved people one knew—family, friends, and acquaintances. He issued a blank piece of paper to each of us and said to list all the people we knew.

I hung onto every word he uttered. But, with no or limited sphere of influence and no advertising capital, my marketing path became clear: attend social activities, distribute flyers, door-knock, and cold-call. Cold calling sounded most efficient. I did not have to spend money or meet a prospect until I learned of potential business. My foreign accent, however, had been a source of frustration since I arrived in the United States. I avoided speaking to people who did not know me until it became necessary.

When the question and answer period came, an urge to ask a question hit me. As it happened many times, I felt bashful. Instead of asking Mr. Q a question, I let others ask as anxiety increased within me. Flashes of how much my accent had affected my life, made my mind jump to the previous year at CNSB. A caller had gone on a tirade when I answered the phone. "I want to speak to someone who speaks English," he had said.

"I speak English," I said.

"No. I want someone who speaks real English. Go do housework or something."

I went quiet as cell-damaging heat swelled within me.

"Can I speak to an American? Let me talk to the manager."

I put the receiver on the desktop, not on hold, so the caller could hear me. I called out to Kathy across the large office and told her, "The man on the phone says he doesn't want to be served by a foreigner!"

"I heard your replies. I'll take the call," Kathy said.

I forwarded the call and watched Kathy listen and speak. She said I was the best person to help the caller with the probate work he wanted done. The caller forwent help rather than deal with a "non-American."

Accent and African were the two obstacles, at the level I operated on, that I had to go through, go around, or jump over if I wanted to break into real estate business. It was worth the trouble— better and more respectable than babysitting or hawking second-hand blouses at the swap meet.

With this resolve, I suppressed my anxiety and raised my hand. When Mr. Q pointed at me, I asked him about cold calling and door knocking.

He crushed my real estate embryo.

"A person with your type of accent should avoid phone contact with prospects until there is business. I recommend you advertise or do mass mailings." He then told the group that cold calling worked for people who spoke with clear, smooth pleasant voices.

By the end of the recruiting session, it was evident I did not fit in Mr. Q's set-up.

Chapter 20

County Job

Even when my dab in real estate faltered, it did not concern me much because, I still had my job at CNSB. Besides, all along, I set my sights on a managerial job in government. The general belief in San Diego, and in Nairobi before I left, had been that government jobs were secure and permanent. Mid-1989, the sentiment remained in vogue. In America, therefore, I longed to work for the city, county, or state of California—the Federal government seemed too far removed.

Private sector jobs paid better, but I had turned my back on them since my stay at the Front Street studio apartment, over two years before. Back then, tired of temp agencies' run-around of a-day-here, a-week-there jobs, I browsed want ads in newspapers and magazines. I spotted an ad by a Wall-Street-type brokerage company for an assistant, a secretarial position—not my choice, but my income would have more than doubled if I got the job. They invited me to an interview. I walked the three blocks from my apartment into a high-rise building on B Street, similar to the ones I imagined working in. I clutched my resume and certificates stashed in a manila envelope next to my handbag.

When I arrived, the ground floor receptionist showed me into a waiting room. After about ten minutes, a tall, thirtyish blonde woman came and asked me to follow her through a corridor into a small sterile meeting room, furnished with a table, black chairs, and a telephone. She told me about the company and about the job—taking dictation, typing, receiving calls and visitors—the usual secretarial stuff. Without asking me about my qualifications or experience, the woman said the boss expected some special treatment.

"Special treatment? What kind of treatment?" What does she mean? My mind indulged me. No! That can't be.

"He gets whatever he wants. He is the top-producer in the company and he is entitled to special perks. If you are not prepared to indulge him, then this isn't the job for you." She looked straight at me and waited for my answer.

I shook my head slowly while I racked my brain for an appropriate answer. I stammered replies. In response, the woman thanked me for attending the interview and escorted me to the reception area without having answered a single job-related question.

With a boss-special-treatment requirement, and my agonizing switchboard experience when the publishing company boss ran me out, I gave-up on private sector jobs. And with the failure of swap meet business and the real estate non-starter with Mr. Q's smooth voice charade, my mind focused on my bedrock—a government job.

City and county jobs had to be different. I applied for any listed administrative vacancy for which I qualified. I attended group tests for the city, county, and post office held in huge halls—like school all over, only bigger. The post office sent me confirmation that they would add my name to their two-year job-waiting list.

The city called. I did several interviews, but my accent got in the way—at least on one occasion I learned about. A supervisor contacted my reference—Ms. Psychologist. She gave a glowing account of my abilities. The supervisor confided in her that she was considering me for a job, but wondered whether with such a heavy accent I could communicate well. Ms. Psychologist confirmed I would be a great employee. She also did what referees should desist from doing—she reported to me about the supervisor's accent concern. When the supervisor called me for another interview, I had decided she was not the supervisor I wanted to work under.

Then county departments called and called. Yoo-hoo! I impressed a three-women-panel at one interview at the San Diego County Assessor's Office, on Pacific Highway. The exact place I longed to work in—a midrise—not a high-rise but a place to build a career, go up the ladder and lock in a healthy retirement package. I did not mind the initial starving wage and basic benefits, similar to CNSB's. My mind looked into the future.

I received a job offer to work as a customer service trainee—giving members of the public information regarding their properties. "*Ngatha*," one of the interviewers was the supervisor. (*Ngatha* is a Gikuyu term for the favorite wife whose approval the husband seeks in major decisions in a polygamous family. Nowadays, people use the name loosely to imply a wife or woman in-charge.)

I was good for the job. Much better, I thought later when I learned, among my colleagues, I was the only one with a college degree. Despite that, I did not fret—start at the bottom and give Ngatha more than her money's worth.

She showed me to my desk, near the counter. Then said to follow her into her office, partitioned with half-glass, half-white particleboards at the west corner of the open office. She went over the office rules. Because of my real estate license, which I believe made them hire me, she asked me to sign a conflict of interest disclosure, stating I would not practice real estate or divulge information I saw in the course of my duties, such as homeowners losing their residences for tax non-payment.

I had already dealt with confidential information on probate matters and distraught homeowners losing their homes at CNSB for two and a half years. Sometimes I had talked to husbands who begged we postpone the auction—that they would get money somehow—because they had hidden the imminent foreclosures from their wives. Or relatives claiming one of them had destroyed a deceased's will or trust. No one heard a peep from me then, not even my co-workers. Ngatha's secrets were safe with me, I told her.

My first job training was to shadow an experienced employee until she, Ngatha, determined I could handle questions on my own. I felt so buoyed and enthusiastic about the job that I would not have minded if she told me to sweep floors for the first week. After dealing with daily deadlines at CNSB, however, it became exceedingly hard for me to pace myself. I sat at one of the front desks. I therefore reached the counter first and waited for my chaperone. I felt stupid when Customers looked at me, expectation in their eyes, while I held them at bay, saying, "Hello, someone will be right up." Meantime, Mrs. Chaperone dragged her feet around other desks to get to the counter. Her long-term status had entitled her to a desk by the back wall, equivalent to a corner office at our level.

On my second week, Mrs. Chaperone was talking on phone when a member of the public arrived at the counter. I made the first misstep because I could not calm myself long enough to wait for my trainer. I directed the customer outside our office to the Property Division, across the hallway where they dealt with appraisals.

Oops! Ngatha could not contain herself. With her shoulder-length hair that encroached on her plump cheeks, I might not have expected her to see me break the rule. What was I thinking? Oh, gosh, it's such a new job—I just got here. She stood, walked to her door, and summoned me with a flashing crook of her index finger. That first finger-flash doomed my job.

Oh, Ngatha. Do not call me that way. That is supposed to be a bad way to call someone. Why? I do not know. It just is. I shuffled to her office, my face crowded with helplessness and remorse.

"Did you understand the rules, or can I repeat them to make sure they are clear?"

"I showed the lady to the Property Division."

"Did you understand you shouldn't answer questions until I say you are ready?"

"Mrs. 'Chaperone' was busy on the phone, and...." Oh, goodness, gracious! I could not think of shutting up, curtsying, and apologizing.

"Have I said you are ready?"

"I'm sorry. I won't do it again." Finally!

How would she tell I was ready to answer questions on my own? In three weeks, the woman had me confused. She should have been glad I had learned the job that fast, was my thinking. The real estate training I had received covered most of the information we gave to customers. A few strokes on a computer keyboard, reading property profiles, and giving information to walk-in members of the public covered the biggest part of my job. A high school diploma holder with some training more than qualified to do what I did. How Ngatha determined I needed over three weeks to train for such a job was beyond me. I also failed to understand why a supervisor would employ someone and kick him or her around within two weeks of a new job. The way Ngatha summoned me, ordered me around, and the tone of her voice, made me resolve to keep clear of her. But how? She, like the legal scale, weighed on one side, and a great future job weighed on the other. How to act to get through probation and progress to a great job remained a mystery, especially because I was not one endowed with the patience to kowtow long enough.

In another week, she beckoned me to her office—palm up, flashing fingers. I just about scratched my head, my eyes dimmed. What did I do now?

"I want you to sort the mail," she said.

I relaxed, before my mind jumped to the lie I told myself, that I could do any job that she assigned me.

"When do you want me to start?" I longed to hear a future date, but our mail had not come in that day.

"Right now. Your colleague will show you how." She pointed to a vibrant skinny young woman, with blonde hair down her backside, seated at one of the lower-rung desks.

Instead of going up the job ladder, I might revert to that housework job to which the caller at the CNSB referred me. Hard to reconcile that years since I left high school, university educated, the best I could do was a mail job. My mind tried to digest that before the vibrant woman joined me.

She led me down a wide stairwell, into the bowels of the building where you could not distinguish day from night. When we reached where we had only walls for listeners, before we arrived at the mail center, she confided in me.

"You better watch out for Ngatha," Miss Vibrant said softly.

"Why?" I mirrored her tone of voice.

"I don't know about her. I survived mail, but the woman after me didn't last."

"You sorted mail?" If she survived, maybe I could.

"Not for long. I was lucky."

"You say to watch out for her. How do I do that? The woman already hates me."

"Just do the best you can. That's all I can tell you."

Miss Vibrant had more advice for me. "I would watch how I dress if I were you." She had overheard rumors that the boss, Ngatha, said my dressing was showy, and that she would put me in my place.

I wore the same office attire from CNSB. But at the County Assessor's office, our department in particular, women came to the office dressed in faded jeans or any casual thing they threw together—like they headed to work in the garden, my late mother would say. Ngatha dressed the same way, a Hawaiian shirt-type blouse with three-quarter sleeves over jeans.

The mail job seemed like punishment. Ngatha and the other interviewers did not mention that the office could relegate me to a lower job than what they promised at the interview. I missed my former job at CNSB.

When I gave notice, Kathy had told me, "You are welcome back if you don't like your new job." But I felt too proud and embarrassed to crawl back on account of the way I gloated about getting a secure county job, which had sounded like an executive job during the interview. I hoped the mail job was just a blip in my career while Ngatha recruited a *suitable* mail person.

*

When I reported to work in the mornings, I followed Mrs. Chaperone to the counter whenever she had to give information to a visitor, while I waited for the people in the basement to sort mail into departmental piles. After I dilly-dallied for about an hour, Ngatha told me to take my break. I felt underutilized and bored, became indignant every time she said I must go on break. I did not answer her, but my face doubled the size of the frowns it assumed the minute I entered the county building.

One day, I talked back. "I just got here. Can I go at ten or eleven?"

"No. Everybody has to follow a schedule, you included."

"I can forgo my break; I don't mind," I pressed on.

I did not know how to occupy myself when I went on 9:00 or 9:30 a.m. breaks. Parked cars surrounded the county building on three sides. The grassy area between the building and parked cars on Harbor Drive, overlooking the San Diego Bay did not excite me either. I could hang around the coffee place at the middle of the building by the two east and west doors (before the administration blocked them for security reasons), but I had eaten breakfast at home, and I did not want to waste a dollar on a drink I did not need.

"No, you can't forgo your breaks."

She quoted labor laws I did not know or care about. Which labor laws said people must go on breaks before they worked? I needed engaging work, not breaks.

At CNSB—my only reference employer in the USA—we took our breaks when we became tired. Sometimes I sat at my desk and read a magazine or a book, or ran a work errand. Not at Ngatha's. With her, or the laws she quoted, it was mandatory to go outside the office.

Half an hour after my break, I went to the basement to get the mail. They sorted mail—hard to say for how long—and put it into the various individual floor carts. My cart contained ground floor departments' mail. When I went to retrieve the County Assessor's cart, as they called it, for the first time alone, the mail sorter told me, "The mail should be ready soon." He asked me what kind of letter I came for.

"I came for the Assessor's cart," I said.

He did a quick appraisal, from my shoes to my hair. "What happened to your mail person?"

"How should I know?" I said. I felt like a caged animal, ready to strike at anyone who came close.

He shot me a look, his mouth shut.

The man dumped piles of mail inside the cart which had departments' names labeled on slots across the top, ready to receive mail as I sorted the pile. I rolled the cart into an elevator and onto the first floor. At our open office, I scooped the mail and heaped it on my desk, the cart beside me. I then sat down, mail opener in hand, slit envelopes open, and placed their contents into the right slots. Ngatha had given me an employee list, similar to the one at the publishing company. She told me to match addresses on envelopes against the names on the list. But most mail came addressed to the County Assessor. I had to determine the right department from the content. If I did not know, Ngatha had said to ask her—too much asking from a person I disliked and feared, and who capped her answers with a snicker, a dig, or a look.

*

One time I pushed the loaded sorted mail cart along the corridor, like a homeless person, only better dressed, pushing a shopping cart. I went door-to-door to the various offices distributing the mail. And who shot from his office yards from me?—Greg Smith, the County Assessor, not a fraction over five-foot-seven, but the highest power in the building. When he reached me, he discreetly eyed me, then the cart, perhaps to match the two of us. A thought crossed my mind. What if I drop on my knees, right now, palms clasped in a prayer stance, bend and make as if to kiss his feet and beg him to transfer me to another department? Courage failed me. Besides, I did not want the do-gooders to think me deranged and hustle me to a 72-hour mandatory observation in a mental slammer. I looked at him with the saddest eyes around and hoped he would notice my gloomy existence.

When going home that evening, I fantasized that one day he would call me to his office and ask me about my troubles. After hearing my story, he would transfer me at once.

My fantasy died unrealized. And my lips remained pouty, my cheeks puffed with simmering anger, day-in and day-out as I sorted mail. I had never done a job where I felt so underemployed, abused, and that angry.

When I got stuck, instead of asking Ngatha as she instructed, I sneaked questions to Miss Vibrant about where to place a confusing letter. Instead of answering me, Miss Vibrant would grab the letter and slip it into the right slot. Other times my mind wandered. I asked myself questions whether I worked so hard to end up a mail sorter, or why I even remained in the United States. At such times, mail got mixed-up without my notice. Even when my mind did not stray, and I believed my sorting flawless, occasionally there appeared a rogue letter. The injured department would shoot a complaint call to Ngatha. I suffered a crook of the finger and a dress-down every time that happened.

*

During a peaceful period, I asked Ngatha how long I would sort the mail.

"Until I get a replacement," she said.

"When do you expect that will be?" The answer "soon," clouded my mind.

"I'm not interviewing. It may take three, six months, or…I don't know. Just do your job. If there's a change, I'll let you know."

If my personality kept to form, I should have counted my days at the County Assessor's Office. Instead, I talked to everyone who witnessed Ngatha mistreat me. Some suggested I talk to her boss. I did. The boss sympathized with me, but said she could not do anything until after my probation. She might then transfer me to another department.

I visited the Human Resources (HR) notice board every few days to check for a job for which I qualified. No luck. A man from the back office advised me to lie low until after probation.

"You don't understand how bad my situation is," I said.

Yes, he understood. He gave me examples of black employees and told me they were there only because they had to feed their families. I watched employees in the huge open back office. Sure enough, the handful of blacks hunched over their desks as if they wanted no one to notice them—lying low. Apparently, they were the only ones who did not have enough members to band into tribal cliques, a theme I noticed with the city and the county.

Up to that point, I had not considered discrimination in Kenya or in the United States. Although I doubted Ngatha mistreated me because we were from different tribes, discrimination became one thing to consider while in America.

Mrs. Chaperone, a motherly-type, told me to do my work and not worry about what Ngatha said. "Tesa," who developed a stammer whenever Ngatha talked to her, said she sympathized with me. "She doesn't like me either," Tesa said. I felt diminished that Tesa had to sympathize with me. The woman was slow by nature, or the job or Ngatha—perhaps both—had terrified her. She asked for help for the simplest things. Other times she said, "I did that wrong, didn't I" even when she had not made a mistake. She lamented, "What will I do if I lose my job?" I guessed that was how she avoided the mail job. Meantime, while Ngatha directed her wrath at me, Tesa, cruised through her probation period "unnoticed." Then I had to put up with her sympathy glances from her secure desk.

*

Through office whispers, or her supervisor, Ngatha learned I was looking for transfer. By then I counted myself lucky if I went for a day without Ngatha stopping at my desk. My mind kept alert expecting anything negative from her. Meantime, a misdirected letter went to the Property Division. Doris went to Ngatha's office to complain in person. Ngatha, with Doris in tow, matched to my desk. She handed me the misdirected letter while she told Doris, "These are the problems I've to put up with."

"I'm sorry," I said, giving a lame excuse about a mix-up. In reality did not know to which office to direct the letter. Good thing Ngatha had scribbled a department's name on the envelope. As the two left, I threw Doris a begging look. For a black woman, I thought she should have known to bring the letter to my desk instead of reporting me. But she may have not known of the tension in our all-women department. Men were the majority in the Property Department where she worked. I then believed, perhaps erroneously, that men would not have involved themselves with such petty animosity.

My conduct could not win me an employee-of-the-week award, but the misdirected letter was over in my mind. Not to Ngatha. After I distributed mail, she called me to her office, offered me a chair across her desk. As soon as I sat down, she said, "You are undermining my job."

I looked at her, not understanding.

"Your intention is to make me look bad, and I won't have it!" She leaned over the desk toward me, poked the desk with her index finger after each word. "…keep this in mind: you found me here and you will leave me right here," she then poked repeatedly toward the chair she sat on.

I had read stories in newspapers of employees complaining about their supervisors, but I never believed a supervisor could go to such length to harass an employee.

*

Two weeks after Ngatha's path crossed mine, my headaches started when I opened my eyes in the morning, when I realized where I would spend my day. They subsided when I returned home in the evening. Within two months, I weighed starving versus going bonkers.

Meantime, the news media reported of another person who had headaches worse than mine, the kind that lead people to take matters into their own hands. The person was reportedly to have armed himself with a gun and returned to a post office that he, allegedly, was fired from in San Diego's North County. Just like at a shooting range, the man target-shot his former supervisor, and I didn't know whom else.

I understood.

I woke up one Friday morning. My headache picked up where it left off the previous night. Today was the day. Decision made, I took my time—showered, dressed, and ate breakfast. I wore blend-in clothes—short-sleeved blouse and a pair of jeans. Ngatha would approve of them. While I contemplated my decision, I recalled the few times I had wished she would get sick or get into an accident on her way to work, and return after my probation and transfer. My mind knew such wishes never materialized. Change had to come from my end. I took a pen and a fresh letter-size paper and wrote a "Dear John" letter to her. Oh, No! I did not put her name. I never wanted to mention her name, write to her, or see her ever again. I addressed the letter to HR.

At about 10:00 a.m. I got in my Ford Festiva and drove from Skyline to 1600 Pacific Highway. As I waltzed to HR office to hand-deliver my resignation letter, my back and shoulders were erect. I was through with slouchy postures. Best of all, my head did not throb at the sight of the county building.

While waiting for my severance papers, I dropped a hint about the understandable little shooting that had taken place in North County. The poor woman and her nearby workmate behaved as if they had just received a bomb threat while strapped to their chairs. She stammered, looked at me, "Don't say that." I became untouchable. First-class service followed, with a promise they would mail my check as soon as the Accounting Department signed it.

Just like that, with no idea what to do next, all my managerial aspirations since my high school days withered and died. My killer headaches died as well.

Chapter 21

Business and Child Rearing

The whole of the Friday I resigned from my county job, I mourned and felt angry for the career that should have been. By the following day, I had had enough of anger—I needed action. I took out the certificates I had accumulated since high school and lay them on my bed. I pegged each to a job. The real estate license seemed the only one useable without those tiring interviews, begging for jobs I knew I could do, but wouldn't get anyway, or having to explain my actions to anyone. I would create and mold my own career. I pumped myself. Maybe selling real estate would finance my travel. Or it would help me save for retirement and buy investment properties.

I recalled the euphoria that washed over me when I purchased my first new bungalow in Nairobi in my twenties. When the developer's agent took me for a final walk-through, I ran my open hand over the walls as I marveled that it was real and all mine. I had looked forward to the same feeling when Esther showed me a foreclosed condo in San Diego in 1988, a year before I encountered Ngatha. Real estate *must* be my destiny.

With a weekly rent of $32.50, a car payment of $159, and a few miscellaneous expenses—health care did not feature in my mind—my savings would last another six months.

The morning of August 15, 1989, I knocked on the door of Realty Edge Ltd. on Plaza Blvd in National City, seven miles from Skyline Hills. Conrad, who had qualified me for the ill-fated condo, had by then opened a real estate office with his wife, Amy. Amy was the broker of record and Conrad was the office manager and trainer. I joined their company as a fulltime real estate agent.

Conrad taught real estate financing once a week. He taught as if he and finance were the same, wrote formulas onto a white board with a black marker, explaining to agents as if they were in graduate school. He never finished a topic at one sitting. When he became tired, or when it got too late in the evening, he stopped. When he resumed the following week, with no notes to remind him, he never started where he left off. It never bothered me because it seemed beyond my immediate needs; I wanted to learn on-the-job basics first.

I soon learned the simple rule in that office, which applied to all other real estate offices: work long hours, work smart, and self-motivate. If you were lazy and failed to follow that simple rule, and became rattled when dusk set-in before you got home, you would be wise to include breadline, or family help, as one of your retirement plans, or a long painful dance with your Miss Ngatha type of supervisor.

*

At the County Assessor's, I craved engaging work. My wishes came to be when I joined Realty Edge, without nag—nag—nag. I read real estate books as if preparing for a marathon. I studied every paragraph of the purchase contract, listing agreement, and other disclosures. I practiced completing sample forms using phantom properties. I knew these forms so well that, if buyers were ready to sign agreements, after I showed them properties, I completed the paperwork on the hood of my car. I kept a stack of real estate forms in folders in a box in the trunk.

I embarked on a seven-day workweek for the next ten years. I prospected: door-knocked, distributed fliers, attended social functions, and cold-called. The first time I knocked on a door, with a chaperone in tow to ensure I did not take flight, I felt light-headed, the kind that precedes fainting. I came into my own gradually.

*

Seven months after I joined Realty Edge Ltd., early 1990, my daughter, Mariana, at eleven years old, received her entry visa from the American Embassy in Nairobi. It had been about four years since I returned to the United States and promised her she would join me later. When mired in school, financial challenges, new business and the immigration process, making alternative living arrangements for her arrival had taken a back seat. Although in reality, I could not afford to rent an apartment. Mariana joined me in Nana's household.

With Fulton Elementary School a walking distance from the house, I figured she would get a feel for American schools in the two last months of the school year. That, coupled with summer months, would acclimate her to the culture and prepare her for middle school.

Nana's boys were then nine and ten. I worried how Mariana would mix with them. She fit-in with the boys, but Nana posed a problem. She complained about Mariana and me speaking in Gikuyu in the house. I let her know I had never spoken a word of English to Mariana, so it was only natural we speak in Gikuyu. Nana took exception. She wanted me to speak in "a language every member of the family can understand."

I explained to her how, even as a grown-up, I became disoriented and homesick when I first arrived in the United States, that after five and a half years, I was still making adjustments. Those ghosts of the loneliness I suffered still haunted me. Despite my explanation, Nana did not—or chose not to—understand culture shock. She claimed that since Mariana had me, she would not be affected. We reached an impasse.

I continued speaking to Mariana in Gikuyu. I also dropped and picked her from school, less than half a mile away. Nana ranted on about that, too. She said Mariana should have walked with the boys and the other neighborhood children.

I stopped offering any more explanations. I dealt with Mariana's situation until I sensed she was ready to join the larger student population.

*

Mariana's coming to America was a happy reunion, but I underestimated the difficulty of raising a child alone without help or extended family. In Kenya, I had my mother and a live-in help. In the United States, the whole responsibility fell on me. The two months Mariana attended Fulton Elementary school, before summer holidays, duped me into thinking it was not as hard as people had led me to believe. When summer came, I searched for an affordable summer program. Any program I learned about had filled to capacity, booked long in advance. By chance, I got a spot for a six-week day camp at Jackie Robinson's YMCA, off Imperial Avenue, about three miles from Skyline Hills.

The rest of the holiday, after the day camp, I dragged Mariana to Realty Edge Ltd where she spent many evenings all the way through middle school. I also took her to other events and parties, cheaper than paying a babysitter—which I would not have done anyway because of the child-abuse horror stories I had heard. We left one party after I learnt it was a childfree party when the host made a snide comment about parents never heeding instructions.

I counted days until school opened in September. Afterward, summer school became a permanent fixture for Mariana, no matter how much she protested that people thought she was dumb because summer school was for those who didn't do well during the school year and had to repeat classes.

*

Mariana did not have many rules she could break. The only thing I called her on was the English dialect she picked from the household: "he do," "I don't want nothin'," "where're you at?," "amount of people...." I told her since English was not our native language, we had to be more respectful of its rules, at least the ones we knew. When she failed to heed my corrections, her punishment was to write the correct version twenty times for every infraction.

Nana aired her opinion by stating that was too harsh a punishment. She thought it had something to do with homework. I did not dare compare it with her sanctioned physical abuse or blame it on the English spoken in her household. Mariana weaned herself from basic grammatical errors and never mangled them again. And the boys suffered no more beatings after Mariana joined and lived in the household for eight and a half months.

MacDonald Dining Hall - USIU (Now Alliant University)

Avenue of Nations - Alliant University (formerly USIU)

Front and side of a bus fare receptacle

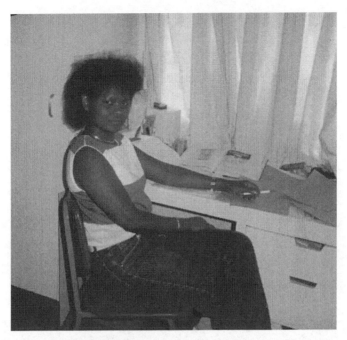

Wanjiru Studying in her bedroom - USIU May 1985

Wanjiru at Mr. Millionaire's balcony.
Atlantic Ocean in the background - Dec 8, 1984

Wanjiru Warama ready for graduation
Civic Center, San Diego, California, June 1985

Wanjiru Warama receiving her diploma from
Dr. William Rust, June 1985

Mary Ann, Dr. Phillips & Wanjiru in front of
Civic Center after graduation, June 1985

Wanjiru Warama with her Graduation Surrogate Mom,
Nancy White Kerch, June 1985

Wanjiru Warama, Kathy Smith, and "Smitty" John W. Smith,
Kathy's then father-in-law

Wanjiru Warama & Dr. Phillips after he addressed a
People to People meeting by USIU Library

Wanjiru receiving her diploma from Dr. William Rust, June 12, 1988

Wanjiru Warama after seven months in real estate, March 1990

Wanjiru Warama Two Years in Real Estate, August 1991

Chapter 22

Homeowner

One of the biggest sales generators in real estate turned out to be "farming," where agents identified neighborhoods, and saturated them with marketing activities. These included distributing flyers, notepads, newsletters, visits, calls, and involvement in the community—until they became household names. The hope was to have homeowners, their families, or friends remember the "farmers" when they thought of purchasing or selling real estate. Some big offices had the various "farms" and their "farmers" highlighted in a map on a wall to avoid overlap, or some agents benefiting from their colleagues' labor.

Besides the hundreds of other doors where I distributed flyers or knocked, I designated about 500 households in the Skyline Hills community as my farm. I distributed flyers and newsletters door-to-door, initially bimonthly and later, once a month. After leaving flyers and newsletters by the door for a year, I then knocked on doors to introduce myself to the homeowners. One day, I knocked on a door that gave me a foothold in California's real estate. The minute the door opened, I started on my sales pitch.

"I'm a real estate broker," the owner said.

I switched to social/business mode. We compared notes on our business experiences, he saying he could not dare knock on anyone's door—he got his business from referrals. "You get business the hard way." He added, "If you get a buyer when you're up and about, maybe you can sell a listing I have problems with."

"What type of house?" I asked.

"It's a three-bedroom, one-and-a-half-bathroom with an attached two-car garage. It needs a little TLC [Tender Loving Care], but it's a nice house."

"How much is it?"

"I have listed it for $88,000."

My ears perked, like a hyena smelling a carcass. I had not come across a house selling below $100,000 near Skyline Hills. "Where is the house?"

"About a mile from here, in North Ridge Terraces." He pointed eastward.

"Where is that?"

"It's between Skyline and Paradise Hills."

"Why is the owner selling?"

"The couple is stationed in Germany. The husband is eager to sell, but the wife is fifty-fifty."

"Why is the man eager to sell?"

"He quit-claimed the house to the wife, and she is now acting up."

"Acting up? What do you mean?"

"He says she developed an attitude since he transferred the house to her. You know how you women can get."

I ignored his innuendo. "Will the wife agree to sign the sales papers?"

"I think so. She agreed to sign the listing agreement."

"Can you show me the house?"

"I will get you the address and tell the tenant to expect you." He entered the house and returned with an address written on a scrap of paper. "Here."

I drove east on Skyline Drive, south on Meadowbrook, and in another turn I came to Arrowwood Drive. The tenant showed me the attached garage, the kitchen, the living room, and the covered patio overlooking a huge backyard. She said she needed a longer notice to show the bedrooms.

I called the listing broker back in two hours after I checked the property's specifications with a title company. I told him the parts of the house I viewed and said, "I got you a buyer."

"Bring me an offer. I'll check when you can show the rest of the house."

"Write it for me. I'm the buyer." It never occurred to me to check with a lender first to ensure I qualified to buy the house.

"Oh, okay. I will write it subject to inside inspection."

"No conditions. I will buy it 'as is.'"

"You got it. I will call you as soon as I write it up."

*

The purchase process dragged—took three weeks to get the offer accepted. The broker gave the tenant a sixty-day notice to vacate; she moved in thirty. In the next two months, whenever the broker called me, he complained about snail mail or Mrs. Seller's reluctance to sign documents. I feared the sale would fall out although with a vacant house the sellers might relent.

In the third month, the broker had termite inspection done and the infested boards replaced. My lender had long approved my loan, as long as the house appraised for at least the price the seller and I agreed. Unknown to me, my lender had already ordered for an appraisal. I learned this when the appraiser called and said the house appraised for $109,000, a $21,000 built-in equity. He congratulated me and said, "You'll do well in real estate." I did not celebrate. By then I had doubts about the broker's ability to complete the sale. His nonchalant, layback attitude bothered me. An independent broker who dressed as sharp as Wall Street executives, but hadn't bothered to pay his Multiple Listing Service (MLS) dues to expose the property to the larger market.

I had no back-up plan if the sale failed to go through. I was eager to move from Nana's house, mainly because I wanted Mariana and I to have our own place. I had already moved out once, and failed, and I was still embarrassed about it.

Four months after Mariana came, tension in the household started building up, about little issues, most of which I do not recall. For one, Nana said I did not trust her babysitting when I took Mariana with me instead of leaving her downstairs with the boys while Nana watched TV in her bedroom upstairs. I did not tell her I would have felt comfortable leaving Mariana if she, Nana, stayed downstairs with the children. To retaliate, Nana got a babysitter for the boys on a Saturday she had to run errands, and I was home.

On another occasion, when we jabbered about finances at her dining table, in front of three women, she told me, "You're a good one to say that [whatever it was]. How would you know? You went through college on a shoestring." I shut up in embarrassment although I wondered how she considered accomplishing something on a "shoestring" negative.

The niggling episodes added up and grated on my mind. I packed Mariana with our belongings in my Toyota Corolla, which I had recently leased, walked out in a huff, and rented a room at the home of elderly Mr. And Mrs. Gardner in Valencia Park. In just a month and a half, to escape Mrs. Gardner's constant need for company and a cooking buddy, I packed our bags again and roomed with Carol, a fellow Kenyan I had housed on a couch at no cost at Nana's for a month. Mariana and I shared one bedroom in the two-bedroom apartment in East San Diego. In three weeks, Carol suffered a mental breakdown. I suspected it was drug and alcohol induced. Although we had got along, she went out with her boyfriend one Saturday and returned to the Winona Street apartment crazed.

At that time, Mariana was asleep in the king bed we shared, and I plopped on a pillow watching TV. At the corridor, Carol talked at the top of her voice while her boyfriend tried to shush her. I believed they were drunk and would calm down and go to sleep, unaware the quarrel was about me. Then Carol rushed into my bedroom, talking at mouth-tripping speed, ordering me to move out that very night. She said she could not stand sharing an apartment with someone who had moved a child twice in less than three months. "The child needs her own bedroom. You got to go," Carol said. Her boyfriend dragged her outside, trying to reason with her; it did not work. She rushed back into our bedroom again, tried to yank one of the posts off the bed several times. Because I ignored her, and the boyfriend kept on interfering, Carol called the police. The police interviewed me exactly where I lay. The only thing one officer did was to switch off the TV.

In less than five minutes, the two officers finished their interview and walked out of my bedroom. They talked to Carol where she waited at the hallway with her boyfriend. Through the open door, I heard them tell her what she was doing was illegal. They said if she did not want me as a co-tenant, she had to give me a 30-day notice. They also said if she did not stop her diatribe, I had the right to file a complaint about her harassment.

After the police left, Carol continued her tirade. It took another hour before she gave up, thanks to her boyfriend. But not before she tried to dismantle the bed we slept in one more time. Her boyfriend pulled her out and forced her into her bedroom. He succeeded that time, and all got quiet in minutes.

The following day, I called Nana and told her I needed a place to stay. Without asking me a single question, she said, "Come on in. You know you're always welcome." I crawled back to her house with my eyes downcast. We settled in as if Mariana and I had never moved out.

By the time I boomeranged to Nana's, the Arrowwood house wallowed in escrow. I did not tell her in case it fell through. To push matters along, I asked the broker I speak to Mr. and Mrs. Seller in Germany. He gave me the phone number. I felt relieved when Mr. Seller answered the phone. I hated to have to speak to Mrs. Seller without knowing what half-truths the broker or her husband had fed her.

"I'm glad you called," Mr. Seller said. "At one time I thought the buyer existed only in my broker's mind." He called the broker incompetent and his wife bigheaded.

"Is your wife okay with the sale?"

"She has come around. If it takes too long, she might change her mind."

"The broker said he is waiting for your wife to sign escrow instructions."

"She wants the appraisal out before she signs the grant deed."

Did Mr. Seller know about the appraisal—the higher amount—and needed time to convince his wife to sign? I did not try to find out—better let the broker handle it.

Instead, I said, "Maybe you can tell your wife the sale is based on our sale agreement, not the appraisal."

"I'll do the best I can. Believe me, I want to sell the house as much as you want to buy it."

"Thank you for your time. Give my regards to your wife."

After a five-month escrow, on January 9, 1991, I became the proud owner of my first house on Arrowwood Drive in Northridge Terraces, a community of San Diego.

A Homeowner in these United States of America! Who would have thought with all the life headwinds I had encountered that I would finish my one remaining year of college, finish graduate school, and become a homeowner.

But, it was just the beginning.

THE END

If you enjoyed reading this book,

please write your comments and rating at

www.amazon.com

This will help other readers find the book.

Acknowledgements

This book would not have turned out the way it is if it weren't for the following people's assistance, support, and suggestions: Members of the La Mesa Writers' Group for allowing me to turn them into my test group, Linda Smith for fostering a nurturing and well-run writers' group, Diana Amsden, Ph.D. who never saw a grammar misstep she didn't frown at, Mary Kelley for her enthusiasm and copy editing and Joe Torricelli for his cheers and believing in my writing before I did. Fredda Durando for her artistic eye, and Dave Fymbo for his skill in translating my ideas into a book cover.

Thanks also go to the brave souls who read the raw manuscript without a hint of complaint: Dr. Tommye Finley, Mary Kelley, John Lee, Kevin Morris, Peggy Roberts, Medicus Washington, Kim Koke, John Githui Warama, Linda Smith, and Heyab Solomon.

I must thank Kathy Davis for speed-reading the sample book and for putting up with my book talk, and finally, but not least, Zion Yohannes who never let me get away with excuses and for her support and friendship.

And I thank you for reading the book and making it all worth it.

Wanjiru Warama